Amelia E. Barr

The Hallam Succession

A Tale of Methodist Life in Two Countries

Amelia E. Barr

The Hallam Succession
A Tale of Methodist Life in Two Countries

ISBN/EAN: 9783337022839

Printed in Europe, USA, Canada, Australia, Japan

Cover: Foto ©ninafisch / pixelio.de

More available books at **www.hansebooks.com**

THE

HALLAM SUCCESSION.

A TALE OF METHODIST LIFE IN TWO COUNTRIES.

BY

AMELIA E. BARR.

NEW YORK:
PHILLIPS & HUNT.
CINCINNATI:
CRANSTON & STOWE.
1887.

Copyright, 1884,

PHILLIPS & HUNT

New York.

TO

MY DEAR FRIEND,

SAM. EARNSHAW WILSON, ESQ.,

THIS TALE

IS, WITH AFFECTIONATE ESTEEM,

INSCRIBED.

PREFACE.

FOR young Methodists in all places and circumstances, I have written this tale: first, to assist them in giving a reason for the faith that is in them; second, to show that they have good cause to love and honor a creed, which not only elevates the most lowly characters, but also adds to gentle birth, wide culture, and noble enthusiasms, beauty, dignity, and grace. A. E. BARR.

CONTENTS.

	PAGE
AMERICANS IN YORKSHIRE	3
MARTHA CRAVEN'S TROUBLE	22
RICHARD AND ELIZABETH	31
WESLEY AND METHODISM	54
ANTONY'S PLANS	70
GOD CLEARS BEN CRAVEN	74
CHRISTMAS	94
RENEWAL OF THE COVENANT	110
SEPARATION	118
AT HOME AGAIN	125
JOHN MILLARD	135
THE PASSIONATE SHOT	143
TEXAS AND LIBERTY	161
RICHARD AT HALLAM	173
MAY, A. D. 1836	177
ANTONY AND HIS BRIDE	190
THE SQUIRE'S DEATH	196
ANTONY'S SIN	209
ELIZABETH'S RESOLVE	221
EVELYN	238
ELIZABETH'S TRIAL	244
LOVE COMFORTED	261
ANTONY'S FATE	266
SANTA FÈ EXPEDITION	271
ELIZABETH IN TEXAS	282
THE SUNSET OF LIFE	297

THE HALLAM SUCCESSION.

CHAPTER I.

> "The changing guests, each in a different mood,
>   Sit at the road-side table and arise:
>   And every life among them in likewise
> Is a soul's board set daily with new food.
>
> "May not this ancient room thou sitt'st in dwell
>   In separate living souls for joy or pain?
>   Nay, all its corners may be painted plain
> Where Heaven shows pictures of some life well-spent."

YORKSHIRE is the epitome of England. Whatever is excellent in the whole land is found there. The men are sturdy, shrewd, and stalwart; hard-headed and hard-fisted, and have notably done their work in every era of English history. They are also a handsome race, the finest specimens extant of the pure Anglo-Saxon, and they still preserve the imposing stature and the bright blonde characteristics of the race.

Yorkshire abounds in what is the typical English home—fine old halls and granges, set in wooded parks, and surrounded by sweet, shady gardens. One of the fairest of these homes is Hallam-Croft. There may be larger halls in the West Riding, but none that combines so finely all the charms of antiquity, with every modern grace and comfort. Its walls are of gray stone, covered with ivy, or crusted with golden lichens; its front, long and low, is picturesquely diversified with oriel windows, gable ends, and shadowy angles. Behind is a steep, craggy range of woody hills; in front, a terraced garden of great extent; full of old-fashioned bowers, and labyrinth-like walks, and sloping down to a noble park, whose oaks and beeches are of wonderful beauty, and whose turf is soft as velvet and greener than any artist ever dreamed of.

Fifty years ago the owner of this lovely spot was Squire Henry Hallam. He was about sixty years of age, stout and fair, and dressed in fine drab broadcloth, with a white vest, and a white cambric kerchief tied loosely round his neck. His hat, drab also, was low-crowned and broad-brimmed, and, as a general rule, he kept it on. In the holy precincts of a church, or if the national anthem was played, he indeed always bared his head; but, in the first case, it was his expression of a religious sentiment, in the second he saluted his country, and, in a measure, himself.

One evening in the early spring he was sitting upon a low sofa in the room that was specially his own, mending some fishing tackle. A couple of setter puppies were worrying each other on the sofa beside him, and a splendid fox-hound leaned her muzzle on one of his broad knees, and looked up into her master's face with sad reproachful eyes. She was evidently jealous, and watching anxiously for some look or word of favor. She had not long to wait. The puppies became troublesome; he chided them, and put the bit of leather they were quarreling about in his pocket. Then he patted the hound, and said: "There's a deal o' difference between them and thee, Fanny, and it's a' in thy favor, lass;" and Fanny understood the compliment, for she whimpered happily, and thrust her handsome head up against her master's breast.

At that moment his daughter, Elizabeth, entered the room. She had an open letter in her hand, and a look half-perplexed and half-pleased upon her face. "Father," she said, "there is a letter from America; Richard and Phyllis are coming; and I am afraid I shall not know how to make them happy."

"Don't thee meet troubles half way; they arn't worth th' compliment. What is ta feared for, dearie?"

"Their life is so different from ours—and, father, I do believe they are Methodists."

The squire fastened the bit of gaudy feather to the trout "fly" he was making, before he answered. "Surely to goodness, they'll niver be that! Sibbald Hallam, my uncle, was a varry thick Churchman when he went to th' Carolinas—but he married a foreigner; she had plenty o' brass, and acres o' land, but I niver heard tell owt o' her religion. They had four lads and lasses, but only one o' them lived to wed, and that was my cousin, Matilda Hallam— t' mother o' these two youngsters that are speaking o' coming here."

"Who did she marry, father?"

"Nay, I knowt o' th' man she married. He was a Colonel Fontaine. I was thinking a deal more o' my own wedding than o' hers at that time. It's like enough he were a Methodist. T' Carolinas hed rebelled against English government, and it's nobbut reasonable to suppose t' English Church would be as little to their liking. But they're Hallams, whativer else they be, Elizabeth, and t' best I hev is for them."

He had risen as he spoke; the puppies were barking and gamboling at his feet, and Fanny watching his face with dignified eagerness. They knew he was going to walk, and were asking to go with him. "Be still wi' you, Rattle and Tory!—Yes, yes, Fanny!— and Elizabeth, open up t' varry best rooms, and give them a right hearty welcome. Where's Antony?"

"Somewhere in the house."

"Hedn't ta better ask him what to do? He knows ivery thing."

There was a touch of sarcasm in the voice, but Elizabeth was too much occupied to notice it; and as the squire and his dogs took the road to the park, she turned, with the letter still open in her hand, and went thoughtfully from room to room, seeking her brother. There was no deeper motive in her thought than what was apparent; her cares were simply those of hospitality. But when a life has been bounded by household hopes and anxieties, they assume an undue importance, and since her mother's death, two years previously, there had been no company at Hallam. This was to be Elizabeth's first effort of active hospitality.

She found Antony in the library reading "The Gentleman's Magazine," or, perhaps, using it for a sedative; for he was either half asleep, or lost in thought. He moved a little petulantly when his sister spoke. One saw at a glance that he had inherited his father's fine physique and presence, but not his father's calm, clear nature. His eyes were restless, his expression preoccupied, his manner haughty. Neither was his voice quite pleasant. There are human instruments, which always seem to have a false note, and Antony's had this peculiarity.

"Antony, I have a letter from Richard and Phyllis Fontaine. They are going to visit us this summer."

"I am delighted. Life is dreadfully dull here, with nothing to do."

"Come to the parlor, and I will give you a cup of tea, and read you cousin Phyllis's letter."

The squire had never thought of asking Elizabeth why she supposed her cousins to be Methodists. Antony seized at once upon the point in the letter which regarded it.

"They are sailing with Bishop Elliott, and will remain until September, in order to allow the Bishop to attend Conference;' what does that mean, Elizabeth?"

"I suppose it means they are Methodists."

The young man was silent a moment, and then he replied, emphatically, "I am very glad of it."

"How can you say so, Antony? And there is the rector, and the Elthams—"

"I was thinking of the Hallams. After a thousand years of stagnation one ought to welcome a ripple of life. A Methodist isn't asleep. I have often felt inclined to drop into their chapel as I passed it. I wonder how it would feel to be awake soul and body at once!"

"Antony, you ought not to talk so recklessly. Some people might imagine you meant what you said. You know very well that the thousand years of 'stagnation,' as you call it, of the Hallams, is a most respectable thing."

"Very respectable indeed! That is all women think about—born conservatives every one of them —'dyed in the wool,' as a Bradford man would say."

"Why do you quote what Bradford men say? I cannot imagine what makes you go among a crowd of weavers, when you might be at Eltham Castle with gentlemen."

"I will tell you why. At Eltham we yawn and stagnate together. The weavers prick and pinch me in a thousand places. They make me dream of living."

"Drink your tea, Antony and don't be foolish."

He shrugged his shoulders and laughed. Upon the whole, he rather liked the look of astonishment in his sister's gray eyes, and the air of puzzled disapproval in her manner. He regarded ignorance on a great many matters as the natural and admirable condition of womanhood.

"It is very good tea, Elizabeth, and I like this American news. I shall not go to the Tyrol now. Two new specimens of humanity to study are better than glaciers."

"Antony, do remember that you are speaking of your own cousins—'two new specimens of humanity'—they are Hallams at the root."

"I meant no disrespect; but I am naturally a little excited at the idea of American Hallams—Americans in Hallam-Croft! I only hope the shades of Hengist and Horsa wont haunt the old rooms out of simple curiosity. When are they to be here?"

"They will be in Liverpool about the end of May. You have two weeks to prepare yourself, Antony."

Antony did not reply, but just what kind of a young lady his cousin Phyllis Fontaine might be he had no idea. People could not in those days buy their pictures by the dozen, and distribute them, so that Antony's imagination, in this direction, had the field entirely to itself. His fancy painted her in many charming forms, and yet he was never able to invest her with any other distinguishing traits than those with which he was familiar—the brilliant blonde beauty and resplendent health of his country-women.

Therefore, when the real Phyllis Fontaine met his vision she was a revelation to him. It was in the afternoon of the last day of May, and Hallam seemed to have put on a more radiant beauty for the occasion. The sun was so bright, the park so green, the garden so sweet and balmy. Heart's-ease were every-where, honeysuckles filled the air, and in the wood behind, the blackbirds whistled, and the chaffinches and tomtits kept up a merry, musical chattering. The squire, with his son and daughter, was waiting at the great open door of the main entrance for his visitors, and as the carriage stopped he cried out, cheerily, "Welcome to Hallam!" Then there was a few minutes of pleasant confusion, and in them Phyllis had made a distinct picture on every mind.

"She's a dainty little woman," said the squire to himself, as he sat calmly smoking his pipe after the bustle of the arrival was over; "not much like a Hallam, but t' eye as isn't charmed wi' her 'ell hev no white in it, that's a' about it."

Antony was much interested, and soon sought his sister.

"If that is Cousin Phyllis, she is beautiful. Don't you think so, Elizabeth?"

"Yes; how perfectly she was dressed."

"That is a woman's criticism. Did you see her soft, dark eyes, her small bow-shaped mouth—a beauty one rarely finds in English women—her exquisite complexion, her little feet?"

"That is a man's criticism. How could you see all that in a moment or two of such confusion?"

"Easily; how was she dressed?"

"In a plain dress of gray cloth. The fit was perfect, the linen collar and cuffs spotless, the gray bonnet, with its drooping, gray feather bewitching. She wore gray gloves and a traveling cloak of the same color, which hung like a princess's mantle."

"How could you see all that in a moment or two of such confusion?"

"Do not be too clever, Antony. You forget I went with her to her rooms."

"Did you notice Richard?"

"A little; he resembles his sister. Their foreign look as they stood beside you and father was very remarkable. Neither of them are like Hallams."

"I am so glad of it; a new element coming into life is like a fresh wind 'blowing through breathless woods.'"

But Elizabeth sighed. This dissatisfaction with the old, and craving for the new, was one of the points upon which Antony and his father were unable to understand each other. Nothing permanent pleased Antony, and no one could ever predicate of him what course he would pursue, or what side he would take. As a general rule, however, he preferred the opposition in all things. Now, the squire's principles and opinions were as clear to his own mind as his own existence was. He believed firmly in his Bible, in the English Constitution, and in himself. He admitted no faults in the first two; his own shortcomings toward Heaven he willingly acknowledged; but he regarded his attitude toward his fellow-man as without fault. All his motives and actions proceeded from well-understood truths, and they moved in consistent and admirable grooves.

Antony had fallen upon different times, and been brought under more uncertain influences. Oxford, "the most loyal," had been in a religious ferment during his stay there. The spirit of Pusey and Newman was shaking the Church of England like a great wind; and though Antony had been but little touched by the spiritual aspect of the movement, the temporal accusations of corruption and desertion of duty were good lances to tilt against the Church with. It gave him a curiously mixed pleasure to provoke the squire to do battle for her; partly from contradiction, partly that he might show off his array of second-hand learning and logic; and partly, also, for the delight of asserting his own opinions and his own individuality.

Any other dispute the squire would have settled by a positive assertion, or a positive denial; but even the most dogmatic of men are a little conscientious about religious scruples. He had, therefore, allowed his son to discuss "the Church" with him, but in some subtle way the older man divined that his ideas were conviction; while Antony's were only drifting thoughts. Therefore, the moral strength of the argument was with him, and he had a kind of contempt for a Hallam who could be moved by every Will-o'-the-wisp of religious or political opinions.

But Elizabeth was greatly impressed by her brother's accomplishments, and she loved him, and believed in him with all her heart. The Hallams hitherto had no reputation for mental ability. In times of need England had found them good soldiers and ready givers; but poets and scholars they had never been. Antony affected the latter character. He spoke several languages, he read science and German philosophy, and he talked such radical politics to the old gardener, that the man privately declared himself "fair cap't wi' t' young squire."

Yet after all, his dominant passion was a love of power, and of money as the means by which to grasp power. Below all his speculations and affectations this was the underlying thought. True, he was heir of Hallam, and as the heir had an allowance quite equal to his position. But he constantly reflected that his father might live many years, and that in the probable order of things he must wait until he was a middle-aged man for his inheritance; and for a young man who felt himself quite competent to turn the axle of the universe, it seemed a contemptible lot to grind in his own little mill at Hallam. He had not as yet voiced these thoughts, but they lay in his heart, and communicated unknown to himself an atmosphere of unrest and unreliability to all his words and actions.

It was soon evident that there would be little sympathy between Richard and Antony. Richard Fontaine was calm, dignified, reticent; never tempted to give his confidence to any one; and averse to receive the confidences of others; therefore, though he listened with polite attention to Antony's aspirations and aims, they made very little impression upon him. Both he and Phyllis glided without effort into the life which must have been so new to them; and in less than a week, Hallam had settled happily down to its fresh conditions. But nothing had been just as Antony expected. Phyllis was very lovely, but not lovely specially for him, which was disappointing, and he could not help soon seeing that, though Richard was attentive, he was also unresponsive.

There is one charming thing about English hospitality, it leaves its guests perfect freedom. In a very few days Phyllis found this out; and she wandered, unnoticed and undisturbed, through the long galleries, and examined, with particular interest, the upper rooms, into which from generation to generation unwelcomed pictures and unfashionable furniture had been placed. There was one room in the eastern turret that attracted her specially. It contained an old spinet, and above it the picture of a young girl; a face of melancholy, tender beauty, with that far-off look, which the French call *prédestineé*, in the solemn eyes.

It is folly to say that furniture has no expression; the small couch, the faded work-table, the straight chairs, with their twisted attenuated legs, had an unspeakable air of sadness. One day she cautiously touched the notes of the instrument. How weak and thin and hollow they were! And yet they blended perfectly with something in her own heart. She played till the tears were on her cheeks, it seemed as if the sorrowful echoes had found in her soul the conditions for their reproduction. When she went back to her own room the influence of the one she had left followed her like a shadow.

"How can I bring one room into another?" she asked herself, and she flung wide the large windows and let the sunshine flood the pink chintzes and the blooming roses of her own apartment. There was a tap at the door, and Elizabeth entered.

"I have brought you a cup of tea, Phyllis. Shall I drink mine beside you?"

"I shall enjoy both your company and the tea. I think I have been in an unhappy room and caught some of its spirit—the room with the old spinet in it."

"Aunt Lucy's room. Yes, she was very unhappy. She loved, and the man was utterly unworthy of her love. She died slowly in that room—a wasted life."

"Ah, no, Elizabeth! No life is waste in the great Worker's hands. If human love wounds and wrongs us, are we not circled by angels as the stars by heaven?" Our soul relatives sorrow in our sorrow; and out of the apparent loss bring golden gain. I think she would know this before she died."

"She died as the good die, blessing and hoping."

Elizabeth looked steadily at Phyllis. She thought she had never seen any face so lovely. From her eyes, still dewy with tears, the holy soul looked upward; and her lips kept the expression of the prayer that was in her heart. She did not wonder at the words that had fallen from them. After a moment's silence, she said:

"My mother loved Aunt Lucy very dearly. Her death made a deal of difference in mother's life."

"Death is always a great sorrow to those who love us; but for ourselves, it is only to bow our heads at going out, and to enter straightway another golden chamber of the King's, lovelier than the one we leave."

Elizabeth scarce knew how to answer. She had never been used to discuss sacred subjects with girls her own age; in fact, she had a vague idea that such subjects were not to be discussed out of church, or, at least, without a clergyman to direct the conversation. And Phyllis's childish figure, glowing face, and sublime confidence affected her with a sense of something strange and remote. Yet the conversation interested her greatly. People are very foolish who restrain spiritual confidences; no topic is so universally and permanently interesting as religious experience. Elizabeth felt its charm at once. She loved God, but loved him, as it were, afar off; she almost feared to speak to him. She had never dared to speak of him.

"Do you really think, Phyllis, that angels care about our earthly loves?"

"Yes, I do. Love is the rock upon which our lives are generally built or wrecked. Elizabeth, if I did not believe that the love of God embraced every worthy earthly love, I should be very miserable."

"Because?"

"Because, dear, I love, and am beloved again."

"But how shall we know if the love be worthy?"

"Once in class-meeting I asked this question. That was when I first became aware that I loved John Millard. I am not likely to forget the answer my leader gave me."

"What was it?"

"Sister Phyllis," he said, "ask yourself what will your love be to you a thousand ages hence. Ask yourself if it will pass the rolling together of the heavens like a scroll, and the melting of the elements with fervent heat. Ask if it will pass the judgment-day, when the secret thoughts of all hearts will be revealed. Dare to love only one whom you can love forever."

"I have never thought of loving throughout all eternity the one whom I love in time."

"Ah! but it is our privilege to cherish the immortal in the man we love. Where I go I wish my beloved to go also. The thought of our love severed on the threshold of paradise makes me weep. I cannot understand an affection which must look forward to an irrevocable separation. Nay, I ask more than this; I desire that my love, even there assuming his own proper place, should be still in advance of me—my guide, my support, my master every-where."

"If you love John Millard in this way, he and you must be very happy."

"We are, and yet what earthly light has not its shadow?"

"What is the shadow, Phyllis?"

"Richard dislikes him so bitterly; and Richard is very, very near and dear to me. I dare say you think he is very cool and calm and quiet. It is the restraint which he puts upon himself; really Richard has a constant fight with a temper, which, if it should take possession of him, would be uncontrollable. He knows that."

"You spoke as if you are a Wesleyan, yet you went to Church last Sunday, Phyllis."

"Why not? Methodists are not bigots; and just as England is my mother-country, Episcopacy is my mother-Church. If Episcopacy should ever die, Elizabeth, Methodism is next of kin, and would be heir to all her churches."

"And Wesleyans and Methodists are the same?"

"Yes; but I like the old name best. It came from the pen of the golden-mouthed Chrysostom, so you see it has quite an apostolic halo about it."

"I never heard that, Phyllis."

"It is hardly likely you would. It was used at first as a word of reproach; but how many such words have been adopted and made glorious emblems of victory. It was thus in ancient Antioch the first followers of Christ were called 'Christians.'"

"But how came Chrysostom to find a name for John Wesley's followers?"

"Richard told me it was used first in a pamphlet against Whitefield. I do not remember the author, but he quoted from the pages of Chrysostom these words, 'To be a Methodist is to be beguiled.' Of course, Chrysostom's 'Methodist' is not our Methodist. The writer knew he was unjust and meant it for a term of reproach, but the word took the popular fancy, and, as such words do, clung to the people at whom it was thrown. They might have thrown it back again; they did better; they accepted it, and have covered it with glory."

"Why, Phyllis, what a little enthusiast you are!" and Elizabeth looked again with admiration at the small figure reclining in the deep chair beside her.

Its rosy chintz covering threw into vivid relief the exquisite paleness of Phyllis's complexion—that clear, warm paleness of the South—and contrasted it with the intense blackness of her loosened hair. Her dark, soft eyes glowed, her small hands had involuntarily clasped themselves upon her breast. "What a little enthusiast you are!" Then she stooped and kissed her, a most unusual demonstration, for Elizabeth was not emotional. Her feelings were as a still lake, whose depths were only known to those who sounded them.

The conversation was not continued. Fine souls have an instinctive knowledge of times and seasons, and both felt that for that day the limit of spiritual confidence had been reached. But it was Phyllis's quicker nature which provided the natural return to the material life.

"I know I am enthusiastic about many things, Elizabeth. The world is so full of what is good and beautiful! Look at those roses! Could flowers be more sweet and perfect? I always dream of happy things among roses."

"But you must not dream now, dear. It is very near dinner-time. We have had a very pleasant hour. I shall think of all you have said."

But the thing she thought most persistently of was Richard Fontaine's temper. Was it possible that the equable charm and serenity of his mood was only an assumed one? As she went to the dining-room she saw him standing in the great hall caressing two large hounds. In the same moment he raised his head and stood watching her approach. It seemed to him as if he had never seen her before. She advanced slowly toward him through the level rays of the westering sun, which projected themselves in a golden haze all around her. Those were not the days of flutings and bows and rufflings innumerable. Elizabeth's dress was a long, perfectly plain one, of white India mull. A narrow black belt confined it at the waist, a collar of rich lace and a brooch of gold at the throat. Her fair hair was dressed in a large loose bow on the crown, and lay in soft light curls upon her brow. Her feet were sandaled, her large white hands unjeweled and ungloved, and with one she lifted slightly her flowing dress. Resplendent with youth, beauty, and sunshine, she affected Richard as no woman had ever done before. She was the typical Saxon woman, the woman who had ruled the hearts and homes of his ancestors for centuries, and she now stirred his to its sweetest depths. He did not go to meet her. He would not lose a step of her progress. He felt that at last Jove was coming to visit him. It was a joy almost solemn in its intensity and expectation. He held out his hand, and Elizabeth took it. In that moment they saw each other's hearts as clearly as two drops of rain meeting in air might look into each other if they had life.

Yet they spoke only of the most trivial things—the

dogs, and the weather, and Richard's ride to Leeds, and the stumbling of Antony's horse. "We left the Squire in the village," said Richard. "A woman who was apparently in very great trouble called him."

"A woman who lives in a cottage covered with clematis?"

"I think so."

"It must have been Martha Craven. I wonder what is the matter!" and they walked together to the open door. The squire had just alighted from his horse, and was talking earnestly to his favorite servant. He seemed to be in trouble, and he was not the man to keep either sorrow or joy to himself. "Elizabeth! my word, but I'm bothered! Here's Jonathan Clough murdered, and Ben Craven under lock and key for it!"

"Why, father! Ben would never do a thing like that!"

"Not he! I'd be as like to do it mysen. Thou must go thy ways and see Martha as soon as iver t' dinner is eat. I sall stand by Martha and Ben to t' varry last. Ben Craven murder any body! Hee! I crack't out laughing when I heard tell o' such nonsense."

In fact, the squire had been touched in a very tender spot. Martha Craven's mother had been his nurse, and Martha herself, for many years, his wife's maid and confidential servant. He felt the imputation as a personal slander. The Cravens had been faithful servants of the Hallams for generations, and Clough was comparatively a new-comer. Right or wrong, the squire would have been inclined to stand by an old friend, but he had not a doubt of Ben's innocence.

"What have you done about it?" asked Antony.

"I've been to see Israel Potter, and I've bound him to stand up for Ben. What Israel doesn't know 'bout law, and what Israel can't do with t' law, isn't worth t' knowing or t' doing. Then I went for t' Wesleyan minister to talk a bit wi' Martha, poor body? She seemed to want something o' t' kind; and I'm bound to say I found him a varry gentlemanly, sensible fellow. He didn't think owt wrong o' Ben, no more than I did."

"People would wonder to see you at the Wesleyan's door."

"May be they'll be more cap't yet, son Antony. I'll ask neither cat nor Christian what door to knock at. I wish I may nivver stand at a worse door than Mr. North's, that's a'. What say you to that, then?"

"I say you are quite right, father."

"I'm nivver far wrong, my lad; nobody is that lets a kind heart lead them, and it would be against nature if I didn't stand up for any Craven that's i' trouble."

Phyllis, who was sitting beside him, laid her hand upon his a moment, and he lifted his eyes and met hers. There was such a light and look of sympathy and admiration in them, that she had no need to say a word. He felt that he had done the right thing, and was pleased with himself for doing it. In a good man there is still a deal of the divinity from which he has fallen, and in his times of trial his heart throbs upward.

Dinner was insensibly hurried, and when Elizabeth rose Phyllis followed her. "I must go with you dear; if Martha is a Methodist she is my sister, and she has a right to my sympathy and my purse, if it is necessary to her."

"I shall be glad. It is only a pleasant walk through the park, and Antony and Richard can meet us at the park gates. I think you will like Martha."

Few words were spoken by the two girls as they went in the amber twilight across the green, green turf of the park. Martha saw them coming and was at her door when they stepped inside the fragrant patch which she called her garden. She was a woman very pleasant to look at, tall and straight, with a strong ruddy face and blue eyes, a little dim with weeping. Her cotton dress of indigo blue, covered with golden-colored moons, was pinned well up at the back, displaying her home-knit stockings and low shoes fastened with brass latchets. She had on her head a cap of white linen, stiffly starched, and a checkered kerchief was pinned over her ample bosom.

Even in her deep sorrow and anxiety her broad

sweet mouth could not forget its trick of smiling. "Come this ways in, Joy," she said to Elizabeth, at the same moment dropping a courtesy to Phyllis, an old-fashioned token of respect, which had no particle of servility in it.

"This is my cousin, Miss Fontaine, from America, Martha."

"Well, I'm sure I'm right suited at meeting her. Mother used to talk above a bit about Sibbald Hallam as crossed t' seas. She looked for him to come back again. But he nivver came."

"I am his granddaughter. I am very sorry, Sister Martha, to hear of your trouble."

"Why-a! Is ta a Methodist, dearie?"

Phyllis nodded brightly and took her hand.

"Well I nivver! But I'm fain and glad! And as for trouble, I'll not fear it. Why should I, wi' t' love o' God and t' love o' man to help me?"

"When did it happen, Martha?"

"Last night, Miss Hallam. My Ben and Jonathan Clough wern't as good friends as might be. There's a lass at t' bottom o' t' trouble; there's allays that. She's a good lass enough, but good 'uns mak' as much trouble as t' bad 'uns sometimes, I think. It's Jonathan's daughter, Mary. She's ta'en Ben's fancy, and she's ta'en Bill Laycock's fancy, too. T' lass likes my Ben, and Clough he liked Laycock; for Laycock is t' blacksmith now, and owns t' forge, and t' house behind it. My Ben is nobbut Clough's overlooker."

"It is a pity he stopped at Clough's mill, if there was ill-feeling between them."

"T' lad's none to blame for that. Clough is makkin' some new kind o' figured goods, and t' men are all hired by t' twelvemonth, and bound over to keep a quiet tongue i' their mouths about t' new looms as does t' work. Two days ago Clough found out that Tim Bingley hed told t' secret to Booth; and Clough wer' neither to hold nor bind. He put Bingley out o' t' mill, and wouldn't pay him t' balance o' t' year, and somehow he took t' notion that Ben was in t' affair. Ben's none so mean as that, I'm sure."

"But Bingley is a very bad man. My father sent him to the tread-mill last year for a brutal assault. He is quite capable of murder. Has no one looked for him?"

"Bingley says he saw my Ben shoot Clough, and Clough says it was Ben."

"Then Clough is still alive?"

"Ay, but he'll die ere morning. T' magistrates hev been wi' him, and he swears positive that Ben Craven shot him."

"Where was Ben last night?"

"He came from t' mill at six o'clock, and hed a cup o' tea wi' me. He said he'd go to t' chapel wi' me at eight o'clock; and after I hed washed up t' dishes, I went to sit wi' Sarah Fisher, who's bad off wi' t' fever; and when I came back Ben was standing at t' door, and folks wer' running here, and running there, and all t' village was fair beside itseln. We wer' just reading a bit in t' Bible, when constables knocked at t' door and said they wanted Ben. My heart sank into my shoes, Miss Hallam, and I said, 'That's a varry unlikely thing, lads; you're just talking for talking's sake.' And Jerry Oddy said, 'Nay, we bean't, dame; Jonathan Clough is dying, and he says Ben Craven shot him.' Then I said, 'He'll die wi' t' lie on his lips if he says that, thou tell him so.' And Jerry Oddy said, 'Not I, dame, keep a still tongue i' thy mouth, it'll mebbe be better for thee.'"

"Martha! How could you bear it?"

"I didn't think what I wer' bearing at t' time, Miss Hallam; I wer' just angry enough for any thing; and I wer' kind o' angry wi' Ben takkin' it so quiet like. 'Speak up for thysen, lad,' I said; 'hesn't ta got a tongue i' thy head to-neet?'"

"Poor Ben! What did he say?"

"He said, 'Thou be still, mother, and talk to none but God. I'm as innocent o' this sin as thou art;' and I said, 'I believe thee, my lad, and God go wi' thee, Ben.' There's one thing troubles me, Miss Hallam, and it bothered t' squire, too. Ben was in his Sunday clothes—that wasn't odd, for he was going to t' chapel wi' me—but Jerry noticed it, and he asked Ben where his overlooker's brat and cap was, and Ben said they wer' i' t' room; but they wern't there, Miss Hallam, and they hevn't found 'em either."

"That is strange."

"Ay, its varry queer, and t' constables seemed to think so. Jerry nivver liked Ben, and he said to me, 'Well, dame, it's a great pity that last o' t' Cravens should swing himsen to death on t' gallows.' But I told him, 'Don't thee be so sure that Ben's t' last o' t' Cravens. Thou's makkin' thy count without Providence, Jerry;' and I'm none feared," she added, with a burst of confidence; "I'll trust in God yet! I can't see him, but I can feel him."

"And you can hold fast to his hand, Sister Martha; and the darker it gets, you can cling the closer, until the daylight breaks and the shadows flee away."

"That I can, and that I will! Look there, my dearies!" and she pointed to a little blue and white tea-pot on the high mantle-shelf, above the hearth on which they were sitting. "Last night, when they'd taken Ben away, and I couldn't finish t' psalm and I couldn't do much more praying than a little bairn thet's flayed and troubled in t' dark night, I lifted my eyes to thet tea-pot, and I knew t' words thet was on it, and they wer' like an order and a promise a' in one; and I said, 'There! thet's enough, Lord!' and I went to my bed and slept, for I knew there 'nd be a deal to do to-day, and nothing weakens me like missing my sleep."

"And did you sleep, Martha?"

"Ay, I slept. It wasn't hard wi' t' promise I'd got."

Then Phyllis took a chair and stood upon it, and

carefully lifted down the tea-pot. It was of coarse blue and white pottery, and had been made in Staffordshire, when the art was emerging from its rudeness, and when the people were half barbarous and wholly irreligious—one of half a dozen that are now worth more than if made of the rarest china, the " Blue Wesley Tea-pot; rude little objects, yet formed by loving, reverential hands, to commemorate the apostolic labors of John Wesley in that almost savage district. His likeness was on one side, and on the other the words, so often in his mouth, " *In God we trust.*"

Phyllis looked at it reverently; even in that poor portraiture recognizing the leader of men, the dignity, the intelligence, and the serenity of a great soul. She put it slowly back, touching it with a kind of tender respect; and then the two girls went home. In the green aisles of the park the nightingales were singing, and the sweet strength of the stars and the magic of the moon touched each heart with a thoughtful melancholy. Richard and Antony joined them, and they talked softly of the tragedy, with eloquent pauses of silence between.

On the lowest terrace they found the squire— Fanny walking with quiet dignity beside him. He joined Elizabeth and Richard, and discussed with them the plans he had been forming for the unraveling of the mystery. He had thought of every thing, even to the amount of money necessary.

"Have they no relations?" asked Richard, a little curiously. It seemed to him that the squire's kindness was a trifle officious. However lowly families might be, he believed that in trouble a noble independence would make them draw together, just as birds that scatter wide in the sunshine nestle up to each other in storm and cold. So he asked, "Have they no relatives?"

"She has two brothers Ilkley way," said the squire, with a dubious smile. "I nivver reckoned much on them."

"Don't you think she ought to send for them?"

"Nay, I don't. You're young, Richard, lad, and you'll know more some day; but I'll tell you beforehand, if you iver hev a favor to ask, ask it of any body but a relation—you may go to fifty, and not find one at hes owt o' sort about 'em."

They talked for half an hour longer in a desultory fashion, as those talk who are full of thoughts they do not share; and when they parted Richard asked Elizabeth for a rose she had gathered as they walked home together. He asked it distinctly, the beaming glance of his dark eyes giving to the request a meaning she could not, and did not, mistake. Yet she laid it in his hand, and as their eyes met, he knew that as "there is a budding morrow in the midnight," so also there was a budding love in the rose-gift.

CHAPTER II.

"I am with thee, and no man shall set on thee to hurt thee." Acts xviii, 10.

"There I will meet with thee, and I will commune with thee from above the mercy-seat." Exod. xxv, 22.

NO man liveth unto himself. In that green, flowery Eden, with the soft winds blowing in at the open doors and windows, and the white sunshine glorifying every thing, there was the whisper of sorrow as well as the whisper of love. The homely life of the village, with its absorbing tragedy, touched all hearts; for men and women belie their nature when they do not weep with those that weep.

At the close of the London season the Elthams returned to their country home, and there was much visiting and good-will. One evening they were sitting in Eltham drawing-room after dinner. The squire had been discussing the Clough tragedy with great warmth; for Lord Eltham had not unnaturally judged Ben Craven upon the apparent evidence, and was inclined to think his position, whether he was innocent or guilty, one of great danger. Hallam would not see things in any such light. He had lived only in the morally healthy atmosphere of the woods and fields, and the sinful tragedies of life had not been actual to him. True, he had read of them in his weekly paper, but it was a different thing when they came to his own door, and called for his active sympathy.

"Right is right, Eltham," he said, with the emphasis of one closed hand striking the other; and it 'ud be a varry queer thing if right should turn out to be wrong. It'll do nowt o' t' sort, not it."

"But, Hallam, it seems to me that you hev made up your mind that Craven is right—right or wrong—and lawyer Swale told me t' evidence was all against him."

"Swale!" replied the squire, snapping his fingers disdainfully. "Why-a! Swale nivver told t' truth i' all his life, if he nobbut hed t' time to make up a lie. As for Bingley, I wish I hed sent him over t' seas when I hed t' chance to do it—he's none fit to breathe t' air in a decent country."

"But Swale says that Bill Laycock has acknowledged that he also saw Craven in his working clothes running over t' moor just about t' time Clough was shot, and Bill and Craven were at one time all but brothers."

"Ay, ay; but there's a lass between 'em now—what do you make o' that?"

"As far as I can think it out, it's against Craven."

"Then think twice about it, Eltham, and be sure to change thy mind t' second time; for I tell thee, Craven is as innocent as thee or me; and though t' devil and t' lawyers hev all t' evidence on their side, I'll lay thee twenty sovereigns that right 'll win. What dost ta say, Phyllis, dearie?"

And Phyllis, who had been watching his large, kindly face with the greatest admiration, smiled confidently back to him, and answered, "I think as you do Uncle Hallam,

> "'For right is right, since God is God;
> And right the day must win;
> To doubt would be disloyalty,
> To falter would be sin.'"

Hallam looked proudly at her, and then at his opponent, who, with glistening eyes, bowed, and answered: "My dear young lady, that settles the question, here. I wish with a' my heart it did so in ivery court in t' kingdom; but, squire, thou knows little o' this world, I'm feared."

"What by that? I don't want to know. As far as I can judge, t' knowledge of t' world is only an acquaintance wi' all sorts o' evil and unjust things. But come thy ways, Eltham, and let's hev a bit of a walk through t' park. I hear t' cuckoos telling their names to ivery tree, and ivery bird in them, and there's few sounds I like better, if it bean't a nightingale singing."

It was getting late, and the squire's proposition was generally indorsed. The whole party resolved to walk to the park gates, and the carriage and Antony's saddle-horse were ordered to meet them there. It was a delightful evening, full of an indescribable tranquillity—a tranquillity not at all disturbed by the *craik* of the rail in the clover, or the plaintive minor of the cuckoo in the thick groves. Eltham and the squire talked earnestly of the coming election. Phyllis, leaning on Antony's arm, was full of thought, and Richard and Elizabeth fell gradually a little behind them. In that soft light her white garments and her fair loveliness had a peculiar charm. She reminded Richard of some Greek goddess full of grace and large serenity. He had resolved not to tell her how dear she was to him until he had better prepared the way for such a declaration; but when the time comes the full heart must speak, though it be only to call the beloved one's name. And this was at first all Richard could say:

"Elizabeth! Dear Elizabeth!"

She recognized the voice. It was as if her soul had been waiting for it. From the sweetest depths of her consciousness she whispered "Richard," and with the word made over her full heart to him. They stood one wonderful moment looking at each other, then he drew her to his breast and kissed her. The sweetest strongest words of love were never written. They are not translatable in earthly language. Richard was dumb with happiness, and Elizabeth understood the silence. As they rode home and sauntered up the terraces, Antony said, "What a dull evening we have had;" but Phyllis was of the initiated, and knew better. She looked at Elizabeth and smiled brightly, while Richard clasped tighter the dear hand he was holding.

About an hour later Phyllis went to Elizabeth's room. It was a large chamber open to the east and south, with polished oaken floors, and hung with white dimity. She sat at one of the open southern windows, and the wind, which gently moved the snowy curtains, brought in with it the scent of bleaching clover. There was no light but that shadow of twilight which, in English summers, lingers until it is lost in the dawning. But it was quite sufficient. She turned her face to meet Phyllis, and Phyllis kissed her, and said,

"I know, Elizabeth; and I am so glad."

"Richard told you?"

"No, indeed! Richard is too much astonished at his own happiness to speak of it to-night. But when one loves, one understands naturally. It has made me very happy. Why, Elizabeth, you are weeping!"

"I am strangely sorrowful, Phyllis. A shadow which I cannot account for chills me. You know that I am neither imaginative nor sentimental; but I am weeping to-night for grief which I apprehend, but which does not exist."

"Why do that? The ills that never come are just the ills that give us the sorest and most useless sorrow. They are not provided for—no grace is promised for them."

"That may be, Phyllis, but these intangible griefs are very real ones while they haunt us."

"I once knew a Methodist preacher who, whenever he felt himself haunted by prospective cares and griefs, took a piece of paper and reduced them to writing, and so 'faced the squadron of his doubts.' He told me that they usually vanished as he mustered them. Elizabeth, there are more than sixty admonitions against fear or unnecessary anxiety in the Bible, and these are so various, and so positive, that a Christian has not actually a legitimate subject for worry left. Come, let us face your trouble. Is it because in marrying Richard you will have to give up this beautiful home?"

"That possibility faces me every day, Phyllis. When Antony marries, he will, of course, bring his wife here, and she will be mistress. I might, for father's sake, take a lower place, but it would be hard. Father did not marry until his three sisters were settled, but Antony lives in another generation. I can hardly hope he will be so thoughtful."

"Do you fear that uncle will object to your marriage with Richard?"

"No; he is very fond of Richard, and very proud of him. Yesterday he made me notice now strongly Richard resembled Colonel Alfred Hallam, who was the cavalier hero of our family. And the likeness is wonderful."

"Has money any thing to do with it?"

"Nothing."

"Parting with Richard?"

"I think so—the feeling is one of a fear of long or final separation—a shadow like an abyss which neither my love nor my hope can cross. I find that I cannot follow out any dream or plan which includes Richard; my soul stumbles in all such efforts as if it was blind. Now is there any promise for an uncertain condition like this?"

"Yes, dear, there is a promise with a blessing added to it. 'I will bring the blind by a way that they knew not; I will lead them in paths that they have not known: I will make darkness light before them, and crooked things straight.'" Isa. xlii, 16.

"Dear Phyllis, what a little comforter you are! I will be happy. Indeed, I have reason, for I never dreamed of a lover like Richard—and he says it was the merest accident that brought you to Europe this summer."

"Did Richard say 'accident?' Do you know, Elizabeth, I think what men call 'accident' is really God's own part—his special arrangement or interposition. We were going to Saratoga, and then one night Bishop Elliott called, and said he was going to Europe, and as he spoke we received a letter saying the rooms which we had always occupied were not to be had, and the Bishop said, 'Go with me to Europe,' and so in five minutes we had decided to do so. Richard will dislike to return to America without you; have you thought of the many changes you must face? and some deprivations also, Elizabeth. We are not rich. Our home, beautiful in its way, is very different from Hallam Hall; our life altogether is unlike yours."

"I fear nothing of all that, Phyllis. But my marriage until Antony marries is out of the question. I could not leave father until he has another daughter. That is a thing not to be contemplated."

"Ah, Elizabeth, in my selfishness I had forgotten that! I was only thinking that when Richard had you, he could better spare me, and that John and I might have a hope also. But, of course, Uncle Hallam comes first."

"Yes; as long as my father needs me, my first duty is to him."

"Even if it be to the end of his life?"

"That is an event I never dare to call to mind. My soul shrinks back from the thought. A good parent is immortal to a good child, I think."

She said it very calmly, but no one would have thought of disputing her position. The still assured face partially uplifted, and the large white hands firmly clasped upon her knee, were a kind of silent amen to it.

"Then Phyllis said "Good-night" and went away; but dim as the light was, she took with her a certain sense of warmth and color. The long pink dressing-gown she had worn and the pink rose in her hair had made a kind of glow in the corner of the wide window where she had sat. "How beautiful she is!" The words sprang spontaneously to Elizabeth's lips; and she added to them in her thoughts, "Few girls are so lovely, so graceful, and so clever, and yet she is as pure and unspoiled by the world as if God had just made her."

The formal ratification of the engagement was very quietly done. The squire had a conversation with Richard, and after it went for a long walk in the park. When he next met his daughter he looked at her steadily with eyes full of tears, and she went to him, and put her arms around his neck, and whispered some assurance to him, which he repaid with a hearty "God bless thee, Elizabeth!"

Antony was the least pleased. He had long had a friendship with George Eltham, Lord Eltham's younger son; and among many projects which the young men had discussed, one related to the marriage of Elizabeth. She had, indeed, no knowledge of their intentions, which were on a mercenary basis, but this did not prevent Antony from feeling that Richard had in some degree frustrated his plans. But he allowed himself no evidences of this feeling; he gave Richard his congratulations, and in a merry way "supposed that the kindest thing he could now do for all parties was to choose a wife also."

But very soon he ordered his horse and rode thoughtfully over to Eltham. The Hon. George was in his apartments reading "Blackwood," though there was a riding party gathering on the lawn.

"Are you not going with them?" asked Antony, indicating the laughing group outside with a motion of his hand.

"Not I. I hope to do something more with my life than be my elder brother's lieutenant. Last night I spoke to Lord Eltham concerning our intentions. He thinks well of them, Antony, and promises all the help he can give us."

"I am sorry to tell you, George, that Elizabeth is to marry cousin Fontaine. The engagement is formally made and sanctioned."

"I am very sorry. It is a great disappointment to me."

"You were too dilatory. I advised you to speak to Elizabeth some months ago."

"I tried to do so, but it was impossible to say pretty things to her. I felt abashed if I tried to compliment her, and she always appeared so unconscious of a fellow, that it was depressing."

"Well, it is too late now."

"How do you know that? When Mr. Fontaine has gone—"

"It will not make a particle of difference, George; let me tell you that. Elizabeth will be true to him, if she never sees him again. I know her, you do not."

"What is to be done, then?"

"I was thinking of Selina Digby."

"O you know she is not pretty at all!"

"We agreed not to let such things as that influence us."

"And she is older than I am."

"She has £50,000, that is more than double Elizabeth's fortune. A man can't have every thing. It is entirely at her own disposal also. Your brother-in-law is far too much absorbed in politics to interfere—the ground there is clear for you."

"If I succeed?"

"I will promise to find capital equal to yours. What did my lord say concerning our plan?"

"He said we must have some instruction, and that he would speak to Sir Thomas Harrington. My father secured his seat in Parliament, and he is sure to allow us to enter his house. We shall have every facility there for acquiring a rapid practical knowledge of banking and finance. I told father it was that or the colonies. I have no idea of being 'only Lord Francis's brother.'"

"Money is the axle on which the world turns, George. When you and I have it we can buy titles—if we want them."

The fever of fortune-making had seized both young men. They were ambitious in the most personal sense of the word. George's position as younger son constantly mortified him. He had had dreams of obtaining honor both as a scholar and a soldier, but he had satisfied himself that for one career he had not the mental ability, and for the other neither the physical courage nor endurance necessary. Of mere rank he was not envious. He had lived among noblemen, and familiarity had bred its usual consequence. But he did want money. He fully recognized that gold entered every earthly gate, and he felt within himself the capacity for its acquirement. He had also precedents for this determination which seemed to justify it. The Duke of Norham's younger son had a share in an immense brewery and wielded a power far beyond that of his elder brother, who was simply waiting for a dukedom. Lord Egremont, a younger son of the Earl of Soho, controlled large amounts of railway stock, and it was said held a mortgage on the family castle. To prove to his father and mother that no law of primogeniture could disinherit him, appeared to George Eltham an object worth striving for.

With these thoughts simmering in his heart he met Antony Hallam at Oxford. They speedily became friends. Antony wanted money also. But in him the craving arose from a more domineering ambition. He wished to rule men, to be first everywhere. He despised the simple provincial title to which he was born, and the hall, with all its sweet gray antiquity, was only a dull prison. He compared its mediæval strength, its long narrow lattices, its low rambling rooms, its Saxon simplicity, with the grand mansions of modern date in which he visited. It must be remembered that it is only recently old houses and old furniture and early English have become fashionable. Antony's dream of a home was not of Hallam, but of a grander Eltham castle, whose rooms should be twice as large and lofty and splendid.

He would control men through their idol, gold; he would buy some old earldom, and have orders and honors thrust upon him. His long, honorable descent would be a good foundation to build upon. He told himself that the Hallams ought to have built upon it generations ago. He almost despised his ancestors for the simple lives they had led. He could not endure to think of himself sitting down as squire Hallam and ruling a few cottagers and tilling a few hundred acres. In George Eltham he found a kindred spirit. They might work for different motives, but gold was the aim of both.

Many plans had been entertained and discussed, but they had finally settled upon a co-partnership in finance. They would discount bills, make advances, and secure government contracts. The latter was the special aim of Antony's desires. But they were not foolish enough to think they could succeed without some preliminary initiation, and this they proposed to acquire in the great banking house of Sir Thomas Harrington, M. P. Lord Eltham had approved the plan. It now remained to secure the squire's agreement and co-operation. As for the money necessary,

George Eltham proposed to acquire it by marriage. Antony had his own plan; he was only waiting until the Fontaines' visit was over, and "that contemptible Craven affair settled."

For he saw plainly that for the time the squire's mind was full of outside interests, and when Antony discussed a subject so vital to himself, he was resolved his father should be in a position to feel its importance, and give it his undivided attention. Personally he had no ill-feeling toward Ben Craven, but he was annoyed at the intrusion of so vulgar an object of sympathy into his home. The squire's advocacy at Eltham had irritated him. He was quietly angry at Elizabeth and Phyllis daily visiting the dame. And when the Methodist preacher had been twice to Hallam to see the squire on the subject, he could not treat the affair with his usual tolerant indifference.

"I have changed my mind," he said, one evening, with that smiling positiveness which is so aggravating; "I am very much inclined to believe that Ben Craven did kill Clough."

The squire looked at him, first with amazement, then with anger, and asked, "When did ta lose thy good sense, and thy good-will, son Antony?"

"I had a talk with Swale to-day, and in his judgment—"

"Thou knows what I think o' Swale. Was there ever a bigger old cheat than he is? I'll put my heart afore Swale's judgment, Ben Craven's all right."

"He will have strong evidence and a clever lawyer against him. He is sure to be convicted."

"Don't thee reckon to know so much. Ben's got a clever lawyer, too; but if he'd nobbut God and his mother to plead for him, his cause 'ud be in varry good hands, thou may be sure o' that."

"I am only saying, father, what Swale says everywhere."

"I'll warrant he'll talk. There's no tax on lying. My word, if there was, Swale 'd hev to keep his mouth shut."

"I cannot imagine, father, what makes you trouble yourself so much about the Cravens."

"Thou can't, can't ta? Then thou canst imagine gratitude for faithful service given cheerfully for three hundred years. Why-a lad, 'twas a Craven saved Alfred Hallam's life at Worcester fight."

"I suppose he paid him for the service. Any how the debt is not ours."

"Ay, is it. It's my debt, and it's thine, too. Ben may live to do thee a service for aught thou knows."

Antony smiled contemptuously, and the squire continued, almost angrily, "There's things more unlikely; look here, my lad, nivver spit in any well; thou may hev to drink of t' water."

When the words were said the squire was sorry for them. They had come from his lips in that forceful prophetic way some speeches take, and they made an unpleasant impression on both father and son; just such an impression as a bad dream leaves, which yet seems to be wholly irrelevant and unaccountable.

Craven was in Leeds jail, and the trial was fixed for the summer term. All things may be better borne than suspense, and all were glad when Ben could have a fair hearing. But every thing was against him, and at the end of the second day's trial, the squire came home in sincere trouble; Ben had been found guilty, but a conviction of his innocence, in spite of the evidence, seemed also to have possessed the jury, for they had strongly recommended him to her majesty's mercy.

Elizabeth and Phyllis went with sick, sorrowful heart to see the dame. The strain had told upon her before the trial, and she had lost her cheerfulness somewhat. But she had come to a place now where anger and sense of wrong and impatience were past.

"Lost confidence, sister Phyllis," she said; "not I; I hev only stopped reckoning on any man or woman now, be 't queen's sen; and I hev put my whole trust i' God. Such like goings on as we've hed! Paper and ink and varry little justice; but God 'll sort ivery thing afore long."

"The case is to come before the queen."

"That's well enough, Miss Hallam, but I'll tak' it mysen into God's council-chamber—there's no key on that door, and there's no fee to pay either. He'll put ivery thing right, see if he doesn't!"

"And besides, Sister Martha, things may not be as

far wrong as we think they are—may not be wrong at all. God moves in a mysterious way."

"And he needs to, Sister Phyllis. There's many a soul 'ud run away from him, even when he was coming to help 'em, if they knew it was him."

"I understand what you mean, Martha—'as a thief in the night.' He breaks all bars and bursts all doors closed against him when he visits either a soul or a cause. I heard you were at Leeds. Do you mind telling us how things went? The squire will not talk to any one."

"I nivver was one to shut my grief up i' my heart, and let it poison my life; not I, indeed. It seemed to me, though, as varry little fight were made for Ben Clough afore he died; he'd signed a paper, declaring positive as it were Ben who shot him; and t' case were half done when that were said. Then Bingley were sworn, and he said, 'as he were coming ovver t' moor, about half past six, he heard a shot, and saw Ben Craven come from behind a whin bush, and run toward t' village; and a minute after Bill Laycock came in sight; and Ben, he said, ran past him, also; and Laycock looked after Ben, and said to Bingley—'that's Ben Craven; he's in a bit of a hurry, I think.'"

"Was Laycock coming from the moor also?"

"Nay, he was coming from t' village, and was going across t' moor to a knur match on Eltham Common."

"Did Laycock swear to that?"

"Ay, he did. He were varry loth to do it; for

Ben and him hed laked together when they were lads, and been thick as thack iver since, till Mary Clough came between 'em. But I noticed one thing, and I think the jury saw it, too—when Laycock were asked, 'if he were sure it was Ben that passed him,' he turned white to the varry lips, and could scarce make out to whisper, '*Ay, he were sure.*' Then Ben looked at him, and I'll nivver forget that look, no, nor any body else that saw it, and least of a' t' man hes got it."

"You think Laycock swore to a lie?"

"I know he swore to a lie."

"It is a pity that Ben's working-suit has never been found."

"It 'll come to light; see if it doesn't."

"Who spoke for Ben?"

"I did. I told t' truth, and there's none that knows me hes a doubt o' that. I said that Ben came home a bit early. He hed his cup o' tea wi' me, and I told him how bad off Sarah Fisher was; and I said, 'I'll wash up t' tea things, lad, and go bide wi' her till it's chapel time; and so thou be ready to go wi' me.' Before I went out I looked into Ben's room, and he'd dressed himsen up i' his Sunday clothes, and were sitting studying i' a book called 'Mechanics;' and I said, 'Why, Ben! Whatever hes ta put thy best clothes on for?' I knew right well it was for Mary Clough, but I wasn't too well pleased wi' Mary, and so I couldn't help letting him see as he weren't deceiving me; and Ben said, 'Nivver thee mind, mother, what clothes I've on, and don't be too late for t' chapel.'"

"And yet Bingley and Laycock swore that Ben had his working-clothes on?"

"Ay, they sware that."

"You are come into deep waters, Martha."

"Ay, I am; but there's One on t' water wi' me. I hev his hand, and he's none going to let me sink. And good-night to you, dearies, now; for I want to be alone wi' him. He isn't far off; you can tak' t' word of a sorrowful woman that he lets himsen be found, if nobbut you're i' earnest seeking him."

She turned from them, and seated herself before her lonely hearthstone, and Phyllis saw her glance upward at the four words, that even in the darkest night was clear to her—"*In God we trust.*"

"Martha used to be so curious, so gossippy, so well acquainted with all her neighbors, so anxious for their good opinion, that it strikes me as singular," said Elizabeth, "that she seems to have forgotten the whole village, and to be careless as to its verdict. Does sorrow make us indifferent, I wonder?"

"No, I think not; but the happy look at things upon their own level—the earth-level; the sorrowful look up."

Not far from Martha's garden gate they met the Methodist preacher. He was going to see Martha, but hearing of her wish to be alone, he turned and walked with Phyllis and Elizabeth toward the park. He was a little man, with an unworldly air, and very clear truthful eyes. People came to their cottage doors and looked curiously at the trio, as they went slowly toward the hall, the preacher between the girls, and talking earnestly to them.

"Well I nivver!" said old Peggy Howarth, nodding her head wisely, "what does ta think o' that, Jane Sykes?"

"It beats ivery thing! There's Ezra Dixon. He's on his way to a class-meeting, I'll lay thee owt ta likes; Ezra!"

"Well, woman! What does ta want?"

"Does ta see Miss Hallam and that American lass wi' t' preacher?"

"For sure I do. They're in varry good company."

"They'll hev been at Martha Cravens, depend on't. They say Martha taks it varry quiet like."

"Ay, she's none o' them as whimpers and whines. Now if it wer' thee, Peggy, thou'd worrit, and better worrit; as if worritting wer' thy trade, and thou hed to work at it for thy victuals. Martha's none like that. Is ta going to thy class to-night?"

"Nay, then, I'm not going."

"I'd go if I was thee, Peggy. Thou'lt hev thysen to talk about there, and thou'lt not be tempted to say things about t' Cravens thou wont be able to stand up to."

"I'd hev some human nature in me, Ezra Dixon,

if I was thee. To think o' this being t' first murder as iver was i' Hallam! and thou talking as if I ought to buckle up my tongue about it."

"Thou ought; but 'oughts' stand for nothing. To be sure thou'll talk about it; but go and talk i' thy class-meeting wi' Josiah Banks looking i' thy face, and then thou'll talk wi' a kind heart. Do as I tell thee."

"Nay, I'll not do it."

"Thou nivver will disappoint t' devil, Peggy."

Peggy did not answer; she was too much interested in the rector's proceedings. He was actually crossing the road and joining the ladies and the preacher.

"Now, then! Dost ta see that, Ezra? Whativer's coming to folk? Why-a! They're a' going on together!"

"Why not? T' rector's a varry good man. It 'ud be strange if he didn't feel for poor Martha as well as ivery other kind heart. Her trouble hes made a' maks o' Christians feel together."

"If Martha was nobbut a Church o' England woman."

"Dost ta really think that t' rector is cut on that sort o' a pattern? Not he. A man may be a Christian, Peggy, even if he isn't a Wesleyan Methody. Them's my principles, and I'm not a bit 'shamed o' them."

It was quite true; the rector had joined the girls

and the preacher, and they walked on together as far as the park gates, talking of Martha and her great sorrow and great faith. Then the preacher turned back, carrying with him to his little chapel the strength that comes from real Christian sympathy and communion.

"What clear prophetic eyes that Mr. North has," said the rector, as they walked thoughtfully under the green arches of the elms.

"He lives very near to the other world," said Phyllis; "I think his eyes have got that clear far-off look with habitually gazing into eternity. It is a great privilege to talk to him, for one always feels that he is just from the presence of God."

"I have heard that you are a Dissenter, Miss Fontaine."

"O no, I am not. I am a Methodist."

"That is what I meant."

"But the two are not the same. I am quite sure that the line between Dissent and Methodism has been well defined from the beginning."

The rector smiled tolerantly down at Phyllis's bright thoughtful face, and said: "Do young ladies in America study theological history?"

"I think most of them like to understand the foundation upon which their spiritual faith is built. I have found every side study of Methodism very interesting. Methodism is a more charitable and a more spiritual thing than Dissent."

"Are you sure of that?"

"Yes. Dissenters began every-where with showing how fallen was the Church, how unworthy were her ministers; but Methodism began every-where with showing her hearers how fallen they themselves were, and how utterly unworthy. Dissent was convinced that Episcopacy was wrong; Methodism sprang from a sense of personal guilt. Dissent discussed schemes of church government, as if the salvation of the world depended upon certain forms; Methodism had one object, to save souls and inculcate personal holiness. Dissent boldly separated herself from the Church; Methodism clung with loving affection to her mother. Her separation was gradual, and accompanied with fond regrets."

"I like that reasoning, Miss Fontaine."

"Do not give me credit for it; it comes from those who have authority to speak upon such matters. But ought not a young lady to know as much about the origin and constitution of her Church as of her country?"

"I suppose she ought. What do you say, Miss Hallam?"

"That I will begin and study the history of my Church. I am ashamed to say I know nothing about it."

"And I say that I will look into Methodism a little. John Wesley, as a man, has always possessed a great attraction to me. It was a pity he left the Church."

"But he never did leave it. Just as St. Peter and St. Paul and St. John went up to the temple at Jerusalem to pray, so Wesley, until the very last, frequented the Church ordinances. I think he was really a very High-Churchman. He was even prejudiced against Presbyterians; and a very careless reader of his works must see that he was deeply impressed with the importance of Episcopacy, and that he regarded it as an apostolic institution. If he were to return to this world again, he would undoubtedly give in his membership to the American Methodist Episcopal Church.

"But remember how he countenanced field-preaching and religious services without forms."

"Do you think it a sin to save souls out of church? Don't you think the Sermon on the Mount a very fair precedent in favor of field-preaching?"

"Miss Fontaine, you argue like a woman. That question is not in logical sequence. Here come Mr. Fontaine and the squire. I hope some other time you will allow me to resume this conversation."

The squire's face brightened when he saw the rector. "A 'good-evening,' parson. Thou thought I'd be in a bit o' trouble to-night, didn't ta?"

"I knew your kind heart, squire, and that it would be sad for Martha and Ben Craven to-night."

"Ay, to be sure." He had clasped Phyllis's hand in one of his own, and turned round with the party; as he did so, drawing the rector's attention by a significant glance to Elizabeth, who had fallen behind with Richard.

"I am very glad if that is the case, squire."

"Ay, it pleases me, too. But about poor Martha, hev you seen her?"

"She wishes to be alone."

"And no wonder. I'm sure I don't know whativer must be done."

"Perhaps the queen will have mercy."

"Mercy! He'll get a life sentence, if that is mercy. Hanging isn't any better than its called, I'll be bound; but if I was Ben, I'd a-deal rather be hung, and done wi' it. That I would!"

"I think Ben Craven will yet be proved innocent. His mother is sure of it, uncle."

"That's t' way wi' a mother. You can't make 'em understand—they will hang on."

"Yes," said the rector. "Mother-love almost sees miracles."

"Mother-love *does* see miracles," answered Phyllis. "The mother of Moses would 'hang on,' as uncle defines it, and she saw a miracle of salvation. So did the Shunammite mother, and the Syro-phœnician mother, and millions of mothers before and since. Just as long as Martha hopes, I shall hope; and just as long as Martha prays, she will hope."

"Does ta think Martha can pray against t' English Constitution?"

"I heard the rector praying against the atmospheric laws last Sunday, and you said every word after him, uncle. When you prayed for fine weather to get the hay in, did you expect it in spite of all the conditions against it—falling barometer, gathering clouds? If you did, you were expecting a miracle."

"Ay, I told t' beadle, mysen, that there wasn't a bit o' good praying for fine weather as long as t' wind kept i' such a contrary quarter; and it's like enough to rain to-night again, and heigh, for sure! its begun mizzling. We'll hev to step clever, or we'll be wet before we reach t' hall."

The rector smiled at the squire's unconscious statement of his own position; but the rain was not to be disregarded, and, indeed, before they reached shelter the ladies' dresses were wet through, and there was so many evidences of a storm that the rector determined to stay all night with his friends. When Elizabeth and Phyllis came down in dry clothing, they found a wood-fire crackling upon the hearth, and a servant laying the table for supper.

"Elizabeth, let's hev that round o' spiced beef, and some cold chicken, and a bit o' raspberry tart, and some clouted cream, if there's owt o' t' sort in t' buttery. There's nothing like a bit o' good eating, if there's owt wrong wi' you."

The rector and the squire were in their slippers, on each side of the ample hearth, and they had each, also, a long, clean, clay pipe in their mouth. The serenity of their faces, and their air of thorough comfort was a delightful picture to Phyllis. She placed herself close to her uncle, with her head resting on his shoulder. The two men were talking in easy, far-apart sentences of "tithes," and, as the subject did not interest her, she let her eyes wander about the old room, noting its oaken walls, richly carved and almost black with age, and its heavy oaken furniture, the whole brightened up with many-colored rugs, and the gleaming silver and crystal on the high sideboard, and the gay geraniums and roses in the deep bay windows. The table, covered with snowy damask, seemed a kind of domestic altar, and Phyllis thought she had never seen Elizabeth look so grandly fair and home-like as she did that hour, moving about in the light of the fire and candles. She did not wonder that Richard heard nothing of the conversation, and that his whole attention was given to his promised wife.

The squire got the delicacies he wanted, and really it appeared as if his advice was very good medicine. Happiness, hope, and a sense of gratitude was in each heart. The old room grew wonderfully cozy and bright; the faces that gathered round the table and the fire were full of love, and sweet, reasonable contentment. When supper was over Richard and Elizabeth went quietly into the great entrance hall, where there was always a little fire burning. They had their own hopes and joys, in which no heart, however near and dear, could intermeddle, and this was fully recognized. Phyllis only gave them a bright smile as they withdrew. The squire ignored their absence; Antony was at Eltham; for an hour the two little groups were as happy as mortals may be.

The rector had another pipe after supper, and still talked fitfully about "tithes." It seemed to be a subject which fitted in comfortably to the pauses in a long pipe. But when he had finished his "thimbleful" of tobacco, and shaken out its ashes carefully, he looked at Phyllis with a face full of renewed interest, and said,

"Squire, do you know that your niece thinks John Wesley was a High-Churchman?"

"What I meant, sir, was this: Wesley had very decided views in favor of the Episcopacy. He would suffer none to lay unconsecrated hands upon the sacraments; and in personal temperament, I think he was as ascetic as any monk."

"Do you think, then, that if he had lived before the Reformation he might have founded an order of extreme rigor, say, like La Trappe?"

"No, indeed, sir! He might have founded an order, and it would, doubtless, have been a rigorous one; but it would not have been one shut up behind walls. It would have been a preaching order, severely disciplined, perhaps, but burning with all the zeal of the Redemptionist Fathers on a mission."

The squire patted the little hand, which was upon his knee, and proudly asked,

"Now, then, parson, what does ta say to that?"

"I say it would be a very good description of 'the people called Methodists' when they began their crusade in England."

"It is always a good description of them when they have missionary work to do. We have had brave soldiers among the Fontaines, and wise statesmen, also; but braver than all, wiser than all, was my grandfather Fontaine, who went into the wilderness of Tennessee an apostle of Methodism, with the Bible in his heart and his life in his hand. If I was a man, I would do as Richard always does, lift my hat whenever his name is mentioned."

"Such ministers are, indeed, spiritual heroes, Miss Fontaine; men, of whom the world is not worthy."

"Ah, do not say that! It was worthy of Christ. It is worthy of them. They are not extinct. They are still preaching—on the savannas of the southwest—on all the border-lands of civilization—among the savages of the Pacific isles, and the barbarians of Asia and Africa; voices crying in the wilderness, 'God so loved the world, that he gave his only begotten Son' for its salvation. A Methodist preacher is necessarily an evangelist. Did you ever happen to read, or to hear Wesley's 'charge' to his preachers?"

"No, I never heard it, Miss Fontaine."

"If ta knows it, Phyllis, dearie, let him hev it. I'se warrant it 'll fit his office very well."

"Yes, I know it; I have heard it many a time from my grandfather's lips. In his old age, when he was addressing young preachers, he never said any thing else to them. 'Observe,' charged Wesley, 'it is not your business to preach so many times, or to take care of this or that society, but to save as many souls as you can.'"

"Now, then, that's enough. Phyllis, dearie, lift t' candle and both o' you come wi' me; I've got summat to say mysen happen."

'He had that happy look on his face which people wear who are conscious of having the power to give a pleasant surprise. He led them to a large room above those in the east wing which were specially his own. It was a handsome bedroom, but evidently one that was rarely used.

"Look 'ee here, now;" and he lifted the candle toward a picture over the fire place. "Who do you mak' that out to be?"

"John Wesley," said Phyllis.

"For sure; it's John Wesley, and in this room he slept at intervals for thirty years. My great grandfather, Squire Gregory Hallam, was a Methodist—one o' t' first o' them—and so you see, Phyllis, my lass, you hev come varry naturally by your way o' thinking."

The rector was examining the face with great interest. "It is a wonderful countenance," he said; "take a look at it, Miss Fontaine, and see if it does not bear out what I accidentally said about La Trappe."

"No, indeed, it does not! I allow that it is the face of a refined, thorough-bred ecclesiastic. He was the son of the Church."

"Yes; he came, indeed, from the tribe of Levi."

"It is a fine, classical, clearly-chiseled face—the face of a scholar and a gentleman."

"A little of the fanatic in it—admit that. I have seen pictures of grand inquisitors, by Velasquez, which resemble it."

"You must not say such things, my dear rector. Look again. I admit that it is a clever face, and I have seen it compared to that of Richelieu and Loyola, as uniting the calm iron will and acute eye of the one with the inventive genius and habitual devotion of the other; but I see more than this, there is the permeation of that serenity which comes from an assurance of the love of God."

"God love thee, Phyllis! Thou'lt be makkin' a Methodist o' me, whether I will or no. I hed no idea afore there was a' that in t' picture. I wont stay here any longer. Thanks be! It's sleeping-time, missee."

"I should like to sleep in this room, squire."

"Why, then, rector, thou shall. A bit o' fire and some aired bed-clothes is a' it wants. Thou's sure to sleep well in it, and thou'lt hev t' sunrise to wake thee up."

And Phyllis thought, when she saw him in the morning, that he had kept some of the sunshine in his face. He was walking up and down the terrace softly humming a tune to himself, and watching the pigeons promenade with little, timid, rapid steps, making their necks change like opals with every movement. The roofs and lintels and the soft earth was still wet, but the sun shone gloriously, and the clear air was full of a thousand scents.

"How beautiful all is, and how happy you look," and Phyllis put her hand in the rector's, and let him lead her to the end of the terrace, where she could see the green country flooded with sunshine.

"Did you sleep well in Wesley's chamber?"

"I slept very well; and this morning the pleasantest thing happened. Upon a little table I saw a Bible lying, and I read the morning lesson, which was a very happy one; then I lifted another book upon the stand. It was 'The Pilgrim's Progress;' and this was the passage I lighted upon: 'The Pilgrim they laid in a large upper chamber facing the sunrising. The name of the chamber was Peace.' There was a pencil-mark against the passage, and I fancy John Wesley put it there. It was a little thing, but it has made me very happy."

"I can understand."

"God bless you, child! I am sure you can."

CHAPTER III.

"He shall call upon me, and I will answer him: I will be with him in trouble; I will deliver him, and honor him." Psa. xci, 15.

"Alas for hourly change! Alas for all
The loves that from his hand proud Youth lets fall,
Even as the beads of a told rosary!"

THAT very day Richard received a letter from Bishop Elliott. He was going to the Holy Land and wished Richard to join him in Rome, and then accompany him to Palestine. Richard preferred to remain at Hallam, but both Elizabeth and Phyllis thought he ought to respond to the Bishop's desire. He was an aged man among strangers, and, apart from inclination, it seemed to be a duty to accede to his request. So rather reluctantly Richard left Hallam, half-inclined to complain that Elizabeth was not sorry enough to part with him. In truth she was conscious of feeling that it would be pleasant to be a little while alone with the great joy that had come to her; to consider it quietly, to brood over it, and to ask some questions of her soul which it must answer very truthfully.

People of self-contained natures weary even of happiness, if happiness makes a constant demand upon them. She loved Richard with the first love of her heart, she loved him very truly and fondly, but she was also very happy through the long summer days sitting alone, or with Phyllis, and sewing pure, loving thoughts into wonderful pieces of fine linen and cambric and embroidery. Sometimes Phyllis helped her, and they talked together in a sweet confidence of the lovers so dear to them, and made little plans for the future full of true unselfishness.

In the cool of the day they walked through the garden and the park to see Martha; though every day it became a more perplexing and painful duty. The poor woman, as time went by, grew silent and even stern. She heeded not any words of pity, she kept apart from the world, and from all her neigbors, and with heart unwaveringly fixed upon God, waited with a grand and pathetic patience the answer to her prayers. For some reason which her soul approved she remained in the little chapel with her petition, and the preacher going in one day, unexpectedly, found her prostrate before the communion table, pleading as mothers only can plead. He knelt down beside her, and took her hand, and prayed with her and for her.

Quite exhausted, she sat down beside him afterward and said, amid heart-breaking sobs, "It isn't Ben's life I'm asking, sir. God gave him, and he's a fair right to tak' him, when and how he will. I hev given up asking for t' dear lad's life. But O if he'd nobbut clear his good name o' the shameful deed! I know he's innocent, and God knows it; but even if they hang Ben first, I'll give my Maker no peace till he brings the guilty to justice, and sets t' innocent in t' leet o' his countenance."

"'The kingdom of heaven suffereth violence,' Martha, 'and the violent take it by force.' Don't get weary. Christ had a mother, and he loved her. Does he not love her still?"

"Thank you, sir, for that word. I'll be sure and remind him o' her. I'd forget that there was iver any mother but me; or any son but my son."

"Say a word for all other weeping mothers. Think of them, Martha, all over the world, rich and poor, Christian and heathen. How many mothers' hearts are breaking to-day. You are not alone, Martha. A great company are waiting and weeping with you. Don't be afraid to ask for them, too. There is no limit to God's love and power."

"I'll pray for ivery one o' them, sir."

"Do, Martha, and you'll get under a higher sky. It's a good thing to pray for ourselves; it's a far grander thing to pray for others. God bless you, sister, and give you an answer of peace."

Very shortly after this conversation one of those singular changes in public opinion, which cannot be accounted for, began to manifest itself. After Clough's positive dying declaration, it was hardly to be expected that his daughter Mary could show any kindness to her old lover, Ben Craven. But week after week went by, and people saw that she positively refused to speak to Bill Laycock, and that she shrank even from his passing shadow, and they began to look queerly at the man. It amounted at first to nothing more than that; but as a mist creeps over the landscape, and gradually possesses it altogether, so this chill, adverse atmosphere enfolded him. He noticed that old acquaintances dropped away from him; men went three miles farther off to get a shoe put on a horse. No one could have given a clear reason for doing so, and one man did not ask another man "why?" but the fact needed no reasoning about. It was there. At the harvest festivals the men drew away from him, and the girls would not have him for a partner in any rural game. He was asked to resign his place in the knur club, and if he joined any cricket eleven, the match fell to the ground.

One September evening Elizabeth and Phyllis went to the village to leave a little basket of dainties in Martha's cottage. They now seldom saw her, she was usually in the chapel; but they knew she was grateful for the food, and it had become all they could do for her in the hard struggle she was having. The trees were growing bare; the flowers were few and without scent; the birds did not sing any more, but were shy, and twittered and complained, while the swallows were restless, like those going a long journey. Singing time was over, life burning down, it was natural to be silent and to sigh a little.

They left the basket on Martha's table and went

quietly up the street. In a few minutes they met the preacher, but he also seemed strangely solemn, and very little inclined to talk. At the chapel gates there were five or six people standing. "We are going to have a prayer-meeting," he said, "will you come in?"

"It will soon be dark," answered Elizabeth, "we must reach home as quickly as possible."

Just then Martha Craven came out of the chapel. A sorrow nobly borne confers a kind of moral rank. Her neighbors, with respect and pity, stood aside silently. She appeared to be quite unconscious of them. At Phyllis and Elizabeth she looked with great sad eyes, and shook her head mournfully. To the preacher she said, "It's t' eleventh hour, sir, and no answer yet!"

"Go thy ways, Martha Craven. It will come! It is impossible thy prayers should fail! As the Lord liveth no harm shall come to thee or to thine!"

The plain little man was transfigured. No ancient prophet at the height of his vision ever spoke with more authority. Martha bowed her head and went her way without a word; and Elizabeth and Phyllis, full of a solemn awe, stood gazing at the man whose rapt soul and clear, prophetic eyes looked into the unseen and received its assurance. He seemed to have forgotten their presence, and walked with uplifted face into the chapel.

Elizabeth was the first to speak. "What did he mean?"

"He has had some assurance from God. *He knows.*"

"Do you mean to say, Phyllis, that God speaks to men?"

"Most surely God speaks to those who will hear. Why should you doubt it? He changeth not. When God talked with Enoch, and Abraham spoke with God, no one was astonished. When Hagar wandered in the desert, and saw an angel descend from heaven with succor, she was not surprised. In those days, Elizabeth, men whose feet were in the dust breathed the air of eternity. They spoke to God, and he answered them.

"Does Methodism believe that this intercourse is still possible?"

"Methodism knows it is possible. The doctrine of assurance is either a direct divine interposition or it is a self-deception. It is out of the province of all human reason and philosophy. But it is impossible that it can be self-deception. Millions of good men and women of every shade of mental and physical temperament have witnessed to its truth."

"And you, Phyllis?"

"I know it."

How wonderfully certain moods of nature seem to frame certain states of mind. Elizabeth never forgot the still serenity of that September evening; the rustling of the falling leaves under their feet, the gleaming of the blue and white asters through the misty haze gathering over the fields and park. They had expected to meet the squire at the gates, but they were nearly at home ere they saw him. He was evidently in deep trouble; even Fanny divined it, and, with singular canine delicacy, walked a little behind him, and forebore all her usual demonstrations.

Antony was sitting at the hall fire. His handsome person was faultlessly dressed, and, with a newspaper laid over his knee, he was apparently lost in the contemplation of the singular effects made by the firelight among the antlers and armor that adorned the wall. He roused himself when the girls entered, and apologized for not having come to meet them; but there was an evident constraint and unhappiness in the home atmosphere. Even the "bit o' good eating," which was the squire's panacea, failed in his own case. Antony, indeed, eat and laughed and chatted with an easy indifference, which finally appeared to be unbearable to his father, for he left the table before the meal was finished.

Then a shadow settled over the party. Elizabeth had a troubled look. She was sure there had been some very unusual difference between Antony and his father. They soon separated for the night, Elizabeth going with Phyllis to her room for a final chat. There was a little fire there, and its blaze gave a pleasant air of cozy comfort to the room, and deepened all its pretty rose tints. This was to the girls their time of sweetest confidence. They might be together all the day, but they grew closest of all at this good-night hour.

They spoke of the squire's evident distress, but all Elizabeth's suppositions as to the cause fell distant from the truth. In fact, the squire had received one of those blows which none but a living hand can deal, for there are worse things between the cradle and the grave than death—the blow, too, had fallen without the slightest warning. It was not the thing that he had feared which had happened to him, but the thing which he had never dreamed of as possible. He had been walking up and down the terrace with Fanny, smoking his pipe, and admiring the great beds of many-colored asters, when he saw Antony coming toward him. He waited for his son's approach, and met him with a smile. Antony did not notice his remark about the growing shortness of the days, but plunged at once into the subject filling his whole heart.

"Father, George Eltham and I are thinking of going into business together."

"Whatever is ta saying? Business? What business?"

"Banking."

"Now, then, be quiet, will ta? Such nonsense!"

"I am in dead earnest, father. I cannot waste my life any longer."

"Who asks thee to waste thy life? Hev I iver grudged thee any thing to make it happy? Thou hes hed t' best o' educations. If ta wants to travel, there's letters o' credit waiting for thee. If ta wants work, I've told thee there's acres and acres o' wheat on the Hallam marshes, if they were only drained. I'll find ta money, if ta wants work."

"Father, I could not put gold in a marsh, and then sit down and wait for the wheat to grow; and all the wheat on Hallam, unless it bore golden ears, would not satisfy me. George and I are going into Sir Thomas Harrington's for a few months. Lord Eltham has spoken to him. Then George is to marry Selina Digby. She has fifty thousand pounds; and we are going to begin business."

"Wi' fifty thousand pounds o' Miss Digby's money! It's t' meanest scheme I iver heard tell on! I'm fair shamed o' thee!"

"I must put into the firm fifty thousand pounds also; and I want to speak to you about it."

"For sure! How does ta think to get it out o' me now?"

"I could get Jews to advance it on my inheritance, but I would do nothing so mean and foolish as that. I thought it would be better to break the entail. You give me fifty thousand pounds as my share of Hallam, and you can have the reversion and leave the estate to whom you wish."

The squire fairly staggered. Break the entail! Sell Hallam! The young man was either mad, or he was the most wicked of sons.

"Does ta know what thou is talking about! Hallam has been ours for a thousand years. O Antony! Antony!"

"We have had it so long, father, that we have grown to it like vegetables."

"Has ta no love for t' old place? Look at it. Is there a bonnier spot in t' wide world? Why-a! There's an old saying,

"'When a' t' world is up aloft,
God's share will be fair Hallam-Croft.'

Look at ta dear old home, and t' sweet old gardens, and t' great park full o' oaks that hev sheltered Saxons, Danes, Normans—ivery race that has gone to make up t' Englishman o' to-day."

"There are plenty of fairer spots than Hallam. I will build a house far larger and more splendid than this. There shall be a Lord Hallam, an Earl Hallam, perhaps. Gold will buy any thing that is in the market."

"Get thee out o' my sight! And I'll tell Lord Eltham varry plainly what I think o' his meddling in my affairs. In order to set up his youngest son I must give up t' bond on t' home that was my fathers when his fathers were driving swine, the born thralls of the Kerdics of Kerdic Forest. Thou art no Hallam. No son o' mine. Get out o' my sight wi' thee!"

Antony went without anger and without hurry. He had expected even a worse scene. He sat down by the hall fire to think, and he was by no means hopeless as to his demand. But the squire had received a shock from which he never recovered himself. It was as if some evil thing had taken all the sweetest and dearest props of love, and struck him across the heart with them. He had a real well-defined heart-ache, for the mental shock had had bodily sympathies which would have prostrated a man of less finely balanced *physique*.

All night long he sat in his chair, or walked up and down his room. The anger which comes from wronged love and slighted advantages and false friendship alternately possessed him. The rooms he occupied in the east wing had been for generations the private rooms of the masters of Hallam, and its walls were covered with their pictures—fair, large men, who had for the most part lived simple, kindly lives, doing their duty faithfully in the station to which it had pleased God to call them. He found some comfort in their pictured presence. He stood long before his father, and tried to understand what he would have done in his position. Toward daylight he fell into a chill, uneasy sleep, and dreamed wearily and sadly of the old home. It was only a dream, but dreams are the hieroglyphics of the other world if we had the key to them; and at any rate the influences they leave behind are real enough.

"Poor Martha!" was the squire's first thought on rousing himself. "I know now what t' heart-ache she spoke of is like. I'm feared I hevn't been as sorry as I might hev been for her."

Yet that very night, while the squire was suffering from the first shock of wounded, indignant amazement, God had taken Martha's case in his own hand. The turn in Ben's trouble began just when the preacher spoke to Martha. At that hour Bill Laycock entered the village ale-house and called for a pot of porter. Three men, whom he knew well, were sitting at a table, drinking and talking. To one of them Bill said, "It's a fine night," and after a sulky pause the man answered, "It ails nowt." Then he looked at his mates, put down his pot, and walked out. In a few minutes the others followed.

Laycock went back to his house and sat down to think. There was no use fighting popular ill-will any longer. Mary would not walk on the same side of the street with him. It was the evident intention of the whole village to drive him away. He remembered that Swale had told him there was "a feeling against him," and advised him to leave. But Swale had offered to buy his house and forge for half their value, and he imagined there was a selfish motive in the advice. "And it's Swale's doing, I know," he muttered; "he's been a-fighting for it iver since. Well, I'll tak t' £300 he offers, wi' t' £80 I hev in t' house, I can make shift to reach t' other side o' t' world, and one side is happen as good as t' other side. I'll go and see Swale this varry hour."

He was arrested by a peculiar sound in the cellar beneath his feet, a sound that made him turn pale to the very lips. In a few moments the door opened, and Tim Bingley stepped into the room.

"Thou scoundrel! What does ta want here?"

"Thou get me summat to eat and drink, and then I'll tell thee what I want."

His tone was not to be disputed. He was a desperate man, and Laycock obeyed him.

"Thou told me thou would go abroad."

"I meant to go abroad, but I didn't. I got drunk and lost my brass. Thou'll hev to give me some more. I'll go clean off this time."

"I've got none to give thee."

"Varry well, then I'll hev to be took up; and if I'm sent to York Castle, thou'lt hev lodgings varry close to me. Mak' up thy mind to that, Bill Laycock."

"I didn't kill Clough, and thou can't say I did."

Bingley did not answer. He sat munching his bread and casting evil glances every now and then at his wretched entertainer.

"What does ta want?"

"Thou hed better give me a fresh suit o' clothes; these are fair worn out—and £20. I'll be i' Hull early to-morrow, and I'll tak' t' varry first ship I can get."

"How do I know thou will?"

"Thou'lt hev to trust my word—it's about as good as thine, I reckon."

O but the way of the transgressor is hard! There was nothing else to be done. Hatefully, scornfully, he tossed him a suit of his own clothes, and gave him £20 of his savings. Then he opened the door and looked carefully all around. It was near midnight, and all was so still that a bird moving in the branches could have been heard. But Laycock was singularly uneasy. He put on his hat and walked one hundred yards or more each way.

"Don't be a fool," said Bingley, angrily; "when did ta iver know any body about at this time o' night, save and it might be at Hallam or Crossley feasts?"

"But where was ta a' day, Bingley? Is ta sure nobody saw thee? And when did ta come into my cellar?"

"I'll tell thee, if ta is bad off to know. I got into Hallam at three o'clock this morning, and I hid mysen in Clough's shut-up mill a' day. Thou knows nobody cares to go nigh it, since—"

"Thou shot him."

"Shut up! Thou'd better let that subject drop. I knew I were safe there. When it was dark and quiet I came to thee. Now, if ta 'll let me pass thee, I'll tak' Hull road."

"Thou is sure nobody has seen thee?"

"Ay, I'm sure o' that. Let be now. I hevn't any time to waste."

Laycock watched him up the Hull road till he slipped away like a shadow into shade. Then he sat

down to wait for morning. He would not stay in
Hallam another day. He blamed himself for staying
so long. He would take any offer Swale made
him in the morning. There would be neither peace
nor safety for him, if Tim Bingley took it into his
will to return to Hallam whenever he wanted
money.

At daylight Dolly Ives, an old woman who cleaned
his house and cooked his meals, came. She had left
the evening before at six o'clock, and if any thing
was known of Bingley's visit to Hallam, she would
likely have heard of it. She wasn't a pleasant old
woman, and she had not a very good reputation, but
her husband had worked with Laycock's father, and
he had been kind to her on several occasions when
she had been in trouble. So she had "stuck up for
Bill Laycock," and her partisanship had become
warmer from opposition.

It was at best a rude kind of liking, for she never
failed to tell any unkind thing she heard about him.
She had, however, nothing fresh to say, and Bill felt
relieved. He eat his breakfast and went to his forge
until ten o'clock. Then he called at Swale's. He
fancied the lawyer was "a bit offish," but he promised
him the money that night, and with this promise
Bill had to be content. Business had long been
slack; his forge was cold when he got back, and he
had no heart to rekindle it. Frightened and miserable,
he was standing in the door tying on his leather

apron, when he saw Dolly coming as fast as she could toward him.

He did not wait, but went to meet her. "Whativer is ta coming here for?"

"Thou knows. Get away as fast as ta can. There hev been men searching t' house, and they hev takken away t' varry suit Bingley wore at Ben Craven's trial. Now, will ta go? Here's a shilling, it's a' I hev."

Terrified and hurried, he did the worst possible thing for his own case—he fled, as Dolly advised, and was almost immediately followed and taken prisoner. In fact, he had been under surveillance, even before Bingley left his house at midnight. Suspicion had been aroused by a very simple incident. Mary Clough had noticed that a stone jar, which had stood in one of the windows of the mill ever since it had been closed, was removed. In that listless way which apparently trivial things have of arresting the attention, this jar had attracted Mary until it had become a part of the closed mill to her. It was in its usual place when she looked out in the morning; at noon it had disappeared.

Some one, then, was in the mill. A strong conviction took possession of her. She watched as the sparrow-hawk watches its prey. Just at dusk she saw Bingley leave the mill and steal away among the alders that lined the stream. She suspected where he was going, and, by a shorter route, reached a field opposite Laycock's house, and, from behind the hedge, saw Bingley push aside the cellar window and crawl in. He had tried the door first, but it was just at this hour Laycock was in the ale-house.

The rector was a magistrate; and she went to him with her tale, and he saw at once the importance of her information. He posted the men who watched Laycock's house; they saw Bingley leave it, and when he was about a mile from Hallam they arrested him, and took him to Leeds. Laycock's arrest had followed as early as a warrant could be obtained. He sent at once for Mr. North, and frankly confessed to him his share in the tragedy.

"It was a moment's temptation, sir," he said, with bitter sorrow, "and I hev been as miserable as any devil out o' hell could be iver since. T' night as Clough were shot, I had passed his house, and seen Mary Clough at t' garden gate, and she hed been varry scornful, and told me she'd marry Ben Craven, or stay unmarried; and I were feeling bad about it. I thought I'd walk across t' moor and meet Clough, and tell him what Mary said, and as I went along I heard a shot, and saw a man running. As he came near I knew it was Bingley i' Ben Craven's working clothes. He looked i' my face, and said, 'Clough thinks Ben Craven fired t' shot. If ta helps me away, thou'lt get Mary. Can I go to thy cottage?' And I said, 'There's a cellar underneath.' That was all. He had stole Ben's overworker's brat and cap from t' room while Ben was drinking his tea, and Ben nivver missed it till Jerry Oddy asked where it was. At night I let him burn them i' my forge. I hev wanted to tell t' truth often; and I were sick as could be wi' swearing away Ben's life; indeed I were!"

Before noon the village was in an uproar of excitement. Laycock followed Bingley to Leeds, and both were committed for trial to York Castle. Both also received the reward of their evil deed: Bingley forfeited his life, and Laycock went to Norfolk Island to serve out a life sentence.

The day of Ben's release was a great holiday. Troubled as the squire was, he flung open the large barn at Hallam, and set a feast for the whole village. After it there was a meeting at the chapel, and Ben told how God had strengthened and comforted him, and made his prison cell a very gate of heaven. And Martha, who had so little to say to any human being for weeks, spoke wondrously. Her heart was burning with love and gratitude; the happy tears streamed down her face; she stood with clasped hands, telling how God had dealt with her, and trying in vain to express her love and praise until she broke into a happy song, and friends and neighbors lifted it with her, and the rafters rang to

"Hallelujah to the Lamb,
  Who has purchased our pardon!
We will praise him again
  When we pass over Jordan."

If we talk of heaven on earth, surely they talk of earth in heaven; and if the angels are glad when a sinner repents, they must also feel joy in the joy and justification of the righteous. And though Martha and Ben's friends and neighbors were rough and illiterate, they sang the songs of Zion, and spoke the language of the redeemed, and they gathered round the happy son and mother with the unselfish sympathy of the sons and daughters of God. Truly, as the rector said, when speaking of the meeting, "There is something very humanizing in Methodism."

"And something varry civilizing, too, parson," answered the squire; "if they hedn't been in t' Methodist chapel, singing and praising God, they 'ud hev been in t' ale-house, drinking and dancing, and varry like quarreling. There's no need to send t' constable to a Methodist rejoicing. I reckon Mary Clough 'll hev to marry Ben Craven in t' long run, now."

"I think so. Ben is to open the mill again, and to have charge of it for Mary. It seems a likely match."

"Yes. I'm varry glad. Things looked black for Ben at one time."

"Only we don't know what is bad and what good."

"It's a great pity we don't. It 'ud be a varry comfortable thing when' affairs seemed a' wrong if some angel would give us a call, and tell us we were a bit mistaken. There's no sense i' letting folks be unhappy, when they might be taking life wi' a bit o' comfort."

"But, then, our faith would not be exercised."

"I don't much mind about that. I'd far rather hev things settled. I don't like being worritted and unsettled i' my mind."

The squire spoke with a touching irritability, and every one looked sadly at him. The day after Antony's frank statement of his plans, the squire rode early into Bradford and went straight to the house of old Simon Whaley. For three generations the Whaleys had been the legal advisers of the Hallams, and Simon had touched the lives or memory of all three. He was a very old man, with a thin, cute face, and many wrinkles on his brow; and though he seldom left his house, age had not dimmed his intellect, or dulled his good-will toward the family with whom he had been so frequently associated.

"Why-a! Hallam! Come in, squire; come in, and welcome. Sit thee down, old friend. I'm fain and glad to see thee. What cheer? And whativer brings thee to Bradford so early?"

"I'm in real trouble, Whaley."

"About some wedding, I'll be bound."

"No; neither love nor women folk hev owt to do wi' it. Antony Hallam wants me to break t' entail and give him £50,000."

"Save us a'! Is t' lad gone by his senses?"

Then the squire repeated, as nearly as possible, all

that Antony had said to him; after which both men sat quite still; the lawyer thinking, the squire watching the lawyer.

"I'll tell thee what, Hallam, thou hed better give him what he asks. If thou doesn't, he'll get Hallam into bad hands. He has thought o' them, or he would nivver hev spoke o' them; and he'll go to them, rather than not hev his own way. Even if he didn't, just as soon as he was squire, he'd manage it. The Norfolk Hallams, who are next to him, are a poor shiftless crowd, that he'd buy for a song. Now dost thou want to keep Hallam i' thy own flesh and blood? If ta does, I'll tell thee what to do."

"That is the dearest, strongest wish I hev; and thou knows it, Whaley."

"Then go thy ways home and tell Antony Hallam he can hev £50,000, if he gives up to thee every possible claim on Hallam, and every possible assistance in putting it free in thy hands to sell, or to leave as thou wishes."

"He'll do that fast enough."

"Then thou choose a proper husband for thy daughter and settle it upon her. Her husband must take the name o' Hallam; and thy grandchildren by Elizabeth will be as near to thee as they would be by Antony."

"Elizabeth has chosen her husband. He is a son of my aunt, Martha Hallam; the daughter of Sibbald Hallam."

"What does ta want better? That's famous!"

"But he's an American."

"Then we must mak' an Englishman o' him. T' Hallams must be kept up. What's his name?"

"Fontaine."

"It's a varry Frenchified name. I should think he'd be glad to get rid o' it. Where is he now? At Hallam?"

"He is in t' Holy Land somewhere."

"Is he a parson?"

"No, he's a planter; and a bit o' a lawyer, too."

"Whativer does he want in t' Holy Land, then?"

"He's wi' a Bishop."

"Ay? Then he's pious?"

"For sure; he's a Methodist."

"That's not bad. Squire Gregory was a Methodist. He saved more 'an a bit o' money, and he bought all o' t' low meadows, and built main part o' t' stables, and laid out best half o' t' gardens. There nivver was a better or thriftier holder o' Hallam. Ay, ay, there's a kind o' fellowship between Methodism and money. This Mr. Fontaine will do uncommon well for Hallam, squire, I should think."

"If I got Antony to come to thee, Whaley, could ta do owt wi' him, thinks ta?"

"I wouldn't try it, squire. It would be breath thrown away. Soon or later thy son Antony will take his own way, no matter where it leads him. Thou hes t' reins i' thy hand now, tak' my advice, and settle this thing while thou lies. It's a deep wound, but it's a clean wound yet; cut off t' limb afore it begins to fester and poison t' whole body. And don't thee quarrel wi' him. He's a man now, and there hes to be a' mak's o' men to do t' world's work. Let Antony be; he'll mebbe be a credit to thee yet."

"I don't believe, Whaley, thou understands what a sorrow this is to me."

"Don't I? I've got a heart yet, Hallam, though thou'd happen think I've varry little use for it at eighty-nine years old; but I'll tell thee what, instead o' looking at t' troubles thou hes, just tak' a look at them thou hesn't. I nivver gave thee a bit o' advice better worth seven-and-sixpence than that is."

"What does ta mean?"

"I'll tell thee. Thou's fretting because Antony wants to go into business, and to get hold o' as much gold and honor as iver he can put his hands on. Now suppose he wanted to spend a' t' money he could get hold of, and to drag thy old name through t' mire o' jockey fields and gambling houses, and t' filth that lies at t' mouth o' hell. Wouldn't that be worse?"

"Ay, it would."

"And they who hanker after an earldom 'll be varry like to pick up some good things on t' road to it. When ta can't mak' t' wind suit thee, turn round and sail wi' t' wind."

"Thou sees, Whaley, I hev saved a good bit o' money, and I gave Antony t' best education Oxford could hand over for it; and I reckoned on him getting into Parliament, and makkin' a bit o' a stir there, and building up t' old name wi' a deal o' honor."

"Varry good; but *strike t' nail that 'll go!* What is t' use o' hitting them that will only bend and break i' thy hand, and get mebbe t' weight o' t' blow on thy own finger-ends. Go thee home and talk reasonably to thy son. He's gotten a will o' his own—that's a way wi' t' Hallams—and he'll tak' it. Mak' up thy mind to that."

"But children ought to obey their fathers."

"Ought hesn't been t' fashion since iver I remember; and t' young people o' these days hev crossed out Fifth Commandment—happen that's t' reason there is so few men blessed wi' the green old age that I asked for wi' the keeping o' it."

The squire pondered this advice all day, keeping apart from his family, and really suffering very keenly. But toward evening he sent for his son. As Antony entered his room he looked at him with a more conscious and critical regard than he had ever done before. He was forced to admit that he was different from his ancestors, though inheriting their physical peculiarities. They were mostly splendid animals, with faces radiant with courage and high spirits and high health. Antony's face was clearer and more refined, more complex, more suggestive. His form, equally tall, was slighter, not hampered with superfluous flesh, not so aggressively erect. One felt that the older Hallams would have walked straight up to the object of their ambition and demanded it, or, if necessary, fought for it. One was equally sure that Antony had the ability to stoop, to bow, to slide past obstacles, to attain his object by the pleasantest road possible.

He met his father with marked respect and a conciliating manner; standing, with one hand leaning on the central table, until told to sit down.

"Thou can hev what ta wants on thy own terms, son Antony."

"Thank you, sir."

"Nay, I want no thanks. I hev only made t' best o' a bad job."

"I hope you may live to see that it is not a bad job, sir. I intend no dishonor to our name. I am as proud of it as you are. I only desire to make it a power and an influence, and to give it the honor it deserves."

"Ay, ay; thou's going to light thy torch at t' sun, no doubt. I hev heard young men talk afore thee. There is Squire Cawthorpe—he was at college wi' me—what a grand poem he was going to write! He's master o' Bagley fox hounds now, and he nivver wrote a line as I heard tell o'. There's Parson Leveret! He was going to hand in t' millennium, and now he cares for nowt i' t' world but his tithes and a bottle o' good port. Howiver, there's no use talking. Whaley will manage t' business, and when thou art needed he'll go up to London to see thee. As long as thou art young Squire Hallam I shall continue thy allowance; when thou hest signed away thy birthright thou wilt hev £50,000, and niver another pennypiece from Hallam."

"That is just and right."

"And sooner thou leaves Hallam, and better it will be for both o' us, I'm sure. It hurts me to my heart to see thee; that it does,"—and he got up suddenly, and walked to the window to hide the tears that forced themselves into his eyes.

"Shake hands with me, father."

"Nay, I'd rather not."

He had his hands under his coat, behind his back, and he kept them there, staring the while resolutely into the garden, though his large blue eyes were too full to see any thing clearly. Antony watched him a moment, and then approached him.

"Forget, sir, what I am going to do. Before I leave Hallam give me your hand, father, as you would give it to your son Antony."

The squire was not able to resist this appeal. He sunk into his chair and covered his face, saying mournfully: "O, Antony! Antony! Thou hes broken my heart."

But when Antony knelt down by his side, and kissed the hand that lay so pathetically suggestive upon the broad knee, he made no movement of dissent. In another minute the door closed softly, and he was alone—as really a bereaved father as if he stood at an open grave.

Antony's adieu to Phyllis was easily made, but his parting with his sister hurt him in his deepest affections. Whatever of unselfish love he felt belonged to Elizabeth, and she returned to her brother the very strongest care and tenderness of her nature. They had a long conference, from which Antony came away pale and sick with emotion, leaving his sister sobbing on her couch. It is always a painful thing to witness grief from which we are shut out, and Phyllis was unhappy without being able to weep with her uncle and cousins. But it is one blessing of a refined household that sorrow must be put aside for the duties and courtesies of life. The dinner table was set, and the squire washed his face, and put on his evening suit, his long white vest and lace kerchief, and, without being conscious of it, was relieved by the change. And Elizabeth had to rouse herself and take thought for her household duties, and dress even more carefully than usual, in order to make her white cheeks and sorrowful eyes less noticeable. And the courtesies of eating together made a current in the tide of unhappy thought; so that before the meal was over there had been some smiles; and hope, the apprehender of joy, the sister of faith, had whispered to both father and sister, "Keep a good heart! Things may be better than they appear to be."

As the squire rose from the table, he said: "Now,

Elizabeth, I hev something varry particular to say to thee. Phyllis will bide by herself an hour, and then we'll hev no more secrets, and we'll try to be as happy as things will let us be."

Elizabeth was in some measure prepared for what her father had to say; but she was placed in a very unhappy position. She did what was kindest and wisest under the circumstances, accepted without remonstrance the part assigned her. The young are usually romantic, and their first impulses are generously impracticable ones. Elizabeth was not wiser than her years by nature, but she was wiser by her will. For the first few minutes it had seemed to her the most honorable and womanly thing to refuse to stand in her brother's place. But her good heart and good sense soon told her that it would be the kindest course to submit. Yet she was quite aware that her succession would be regarded by the tenants and neighbors with extreme dislike. They would look upon Richard and herself as supplanters; Richard's foreign birth would be a constant offense; her clear mind took in all the consequences, and she felt hurt at Antony for forcing them upon her.

She sat pale and silent, listening to all the squire said, and vainly trying to find some honorable and kind way out of the position.

"Thou must know what thou art doing, Elizabeth," he said, "and must take the charge wi' thy eyes open to a' it asks of thee."

Then he showed her the books of the estate, made her understand the value of every field and meadow, of every house and farm and young plantation of wood. "It's a grand property, and Antony was a born fool to part wi' such a bird in t' hand for any number o' finer ones in t' bush. Does ta understand its value?"

"I am sure I do."

"And thou is proud o' being the daughter o' such land?"

"I love every rood of it."

"Then listen to me. Thy mother gave thee £5,000. It was put out at interest on thy first birthday, and I hev added a £100 now and then, as I could see my way clear to do so. Thou hes now £22,000 o' thy own—a varry tidy fortune. If ta takes Hallam thou must pay down a' of this to Antony. I'll hev to find t' other £28,000 by a mortgage. Then I shall sell all t' young timber that's wise to sell, and some o' Hallam marsh, to pay off t' mortgage. That will take time to do wisely, and it will be work enough for me for t' balance o' my life. But I'll leave thee Hallam clear if God spare me five years longer, and then there 'll be few women i' England thou need envy."

"Whatever I have is yours, father. Do as you think best. I will try to learn all about the estate, and I promise you most faithfully to hold it in a good stewardship for those who shall come after me."

"Give me a kiss, my lass, on that promise. I don't say as a lass can iver be to Hallam what Antony should hev been; but thou 'rt bound to do thy best."

"And, father, Antony is very clever. Who can tell what he may do? If a man wants to go up, the door is open to wit and skill and industry. Antony has all these."

"Fair words! Fair words, Elizabeth! But we wont sell t' wheat till we have reaped t' field; and Antony's wheat isn't sown yet. He's gotten more projects in his mind than there's places on t' map. I don't like such ways!"

"If Antony is any thing, father, he is clear-sighted for his own interest. He knows the road he is going to take, you may be very sure."

"Nay, then, I'm not sure. I'll always suspect that a dark road is a bad road until I'm safe off it."

"We may as well hope for the best. Antony appeared to understand what he was doing."

"Antony has got t' gold sickness varry bad, and they'd be fools indeed who'd consult a man wi' a fever on his own case. But we're nobbut talking for talking's sake. Let us go to Phyllis. She'll hev been more 'an a bit lonely, I'm feared."

A servant with candles opened the parlor door for them. The rector was sitting in the fire-light, and Phyllis softly playing and singing at the piano. She looked up with a smile in her eyes, and finished her hymn. The four lines seemed like a voice from heaven to the anxious father and sister:

> "Judge not the Lord by feeble sense,
> But trust him for his grace;
> Behind a frowning providence
> He hides a smiling face."

"Sing them words again, Phyllis, dearie," said the squire, and as she did so he let them sink into his heart and fill all its restless chambers with confidence and peace.

CHAPTER IV.

"Stir the deep wells of life that flow within you,
  Touched by God's genial hand;
And let the chastened sure ambition win you
  To serve his high command.

"And mighty love embracing al' things human
  In one all-fathering name,
Stamping God's seal on trivial things and common,
  With consecrated aim."

AS the weeks went on the squire's confidence insensibly grew. He met Lord Eltham one day when he was out riding, and they did not quarrel. On the contrary, Eltham was so conciliating, so patient, and so confidently hopeful, that it was almost impossible for Hallam not to be in some measure influenced by him.

"I'm quite sure t' young fellows will succeed," he said, "and if there's more 'an one son i' a family thou may take my word for it it's a varry comfortable thing to hev more 'an one living for 'em."

"And if they spoil t' horn instead o' making t' spoon, what then, Eltham?"

"They'll hev hed t' experience, and they'll be more ready to settle down to what is made for 'em, and to be content wi' it."

"That's varry fine i' thy case, for t' experience 'll

cost thee nothing. Thou is giving thy younger son a chance out o' t' Digby's and Hallam's money."

Eltham only laughed. "Ivery experiment comes out o' somebody's pocket, Hallam—it'll be my turn next happen. Will ta come t' hunt dinner at Eltham on Thursday?"

"Nay, I wont. I'll not bite nor sup at thy table again till we see what we shall see. If I want to say what I think about thee, I'm none going to tie my tongue aforehand."

"We'll be fast friends yet. See if we bean't! Good-bye to thee, Hallam. Thou'lt be going through t' park, I expect?"

"Ay; I'll like enough find company there."

It was about three o'clock, gray and chill. There had been a good deal of snow, and, except where it was brushed away from the foot-path, it lay white and unbroken, the black trunks of the trees among it looking like pillars of ebony in the ivory-paved courts of a temple. Up in the sky winter was passing with all his somber train, the clouds flying rapidly in great grotesque masses, and seeming to touch the tops of the trees like a gloomy, floating veil.

Phyllis and Elizabeth, wrapped in woolens and furs, walked cheerily on, Phyllis leaning upon the arm of Elizabeth. They were very happy, and their low laughter and snatches of Christmas carols made a distinct sound in the silent park, for the birds were all quiet and preoccupied, and flitted about the hawthorns with anxious little ways that were almost human in their care and melancholy. The girls had some crumbs of bread and ears of wheat in a basket, and they scattered them here and there in sheltered nooks.

"I'm so glad you remembered it, Phyllis. I shall never forgive myself for not having thought of it before."

"It is only bare justice to our winged sisters. God made the berries for their winter store, and we have taken them to adorn our houses and churches. Unless we provide a good substitute there is an odor of cruel sacrifice about our festal decorations. And if the poor little robins and wrens die of hunger, do you think He, who sees them fall, will hold us innocent?"

"Look how with bright black eyes they watch us scattering the food! I hope it will not snow until all of them have had a good supper."

Elizabeth was unusually gay. She had had a delightful letter from Richard, and he was to return to Hallam about the New-Year. There had also been one from Antony, beginning "Honored Sir," and ending with the "affectionate duty" of Antony Hallam; and, though the squire had handed it over to Elizabeth without a word, she understood well the brighter light in his face and the cheerful ring in his voice.

They went into Martha's laughing, and found her

standing upon a table hanging up Christmas boughs. The little tea-pot was in a bower of holly leaves, and held a posy of the scarlet hawthorn berries mixed with the white, waxy ones of the mistletoe.

"You wont forget the birds, Martha? You have been stealing from their larder, I see."

"I'm none o' that sort, Miss Phyllis. Look 'ee there;" and she pointed to the broad lintel of her window, which had been scattered over with crumbs; where, busily picking them up, were two robin redbreasts, who chirruped thankfully, and watched Martha with bright curious eyes.

"Mary Clough's coming to dinner to-morrow, and her and Ben are going to t' chapel together. Ben's getten himsen a new suit o' broadcloth, and my word! they'll be a handsome couple!"

"You'll have a happy Christmas, Martha."

"Nobody in a' England hes more reason to keep a joyful Christmas, Miss Hallam."

"No two Christmases are exactly alike; are they, Martha? Last year your daughter was with you. Now she is married and gone far away. Last Christmas my brother was at home. He is not coming this year."

"I found that out long ago, Miss Hallam. First we missed father, then mother; then it was a brother or a sister, or a child more or less; then my husband went, and last year, Sarah Ann."

"Will you and Ben come to the hall to-night?"

"Why—mebbe we will."

"Ben has quite got over his trouble?"

"Ah, Mary helped him a deal."

"Mary will get a good husband."

"She will that. Ben Craven is good at home. You may measure a man by his home conduct, it's t' right place to draw t' line, you may depend upon it. Tak' a bit o' Christmas loaf, and go your ways back now, dearies, for we'll be heving a storm varry soon."

They went merrily out, and about fifty yards away met Mr. North. He also looked very happy, and his lips were moving, as if he was silently singing. In fact, he was very happy; he had been giving gifts to the poor, and the blessing of many "ready to perish" was upon him. He thanked Phyllis and Elizabeth for the Christmas offerings sent to his chapel; and told them of a special service that was to be held on the first Sunday of the new year. "I should like you to be there, Miss Fontaine," he said, "for I think this peculiar service of Methodism is not held in America."

His happiness had conquered his timidity. He looked almost handsome, as he gave them at parting "God's blessing," and the wish for a "Merry Christmas."

"I wish you would ask him to dinner, Elizabeth?"

"Certainly, I will. I should like to do it."

They hurried after him, and overtook him, with his hand upon a cottage gate.

"Will you come and dine with us, Mr. North? It is a gala night at the hall, and many of your people will be there. They will like to see you, and you will add to our pleasure also."

"Thank you, Miss Hallam. It will be very pleasant to me. My duty will be finished in half an hour, then I will follow you."

His face was as happy and as candid as a child's, as he lifted his hat, and entered the cottage garden. Elizabeth involuntarily watched him.

"He seems to tread upon air. I don't believe he remembers he is still in the body. He looks like a gentleman to-day."

"He is always a gentleman, Elizabeth. I am told he has about £70 a year. Who but a gentleman could live upon that and look as he does? Ben Craven has double it, but who would call Ben a gentleman?"

"There is a singular thing about the appearance of Methodist preachers, Phyllis; they all look alike. If you see a dozen of them together, the monotony is tiresome. The best of them are only larger specimens of the same type—are related to the others as a crown piece is related to a shilling. You know a Methodist minister as soon as you see him."

"That is just as it ought to be. They are the Methodist coin, and they bear its image and its superscription. The disciples had evidently the same kind of 'monotony.' People who were not Nazarenes 'took knowledge of them, that they had been with Jesus.' But if this is a fault, surely the English clergy have it in a remarkable degree. I know an Episcopal clergyman just as soon and just as far as I can see him."

"Their cloth—"

"O, it is not only their 'cloth.' That long surtout, and nicely adjusted white tie, and general smoothness and trimness, is all very distinctive and proper; but I refer quite as much to that peculiar self-containedness of aspect and that air of propriety and polish which surrounds them like an atmosphere."

"Now we are quits, Phyllis, and I think we had better walk faster. See what large flakes of snow are beginning to fall!"

The squire had reached home first, and was standing at the door to meet them, his large rosy face all smiles. There was a roaring, leaping fire in the hall, and its trophies of chase and war were wreathed and crowned with fir and box and holly. Branches of mistletoe hung above the doors and the hearth-stone; and all the rooms were equally bright. The servants tripped about in their best clothes, the men with bits of hawthorn berries and box on their breast, the women with sprigs of mistletoe. There was the happiest sense of good humor and good-will, the far-away echo of laughter, the tinkling of glass and china and silver, the faint delicious aroma, through opening doors, of plentiful good cheer.

"Whativer kept you so long, dearies? Run away

and don yourselves, and make yourselves gay and fine. Christmas comes but once a year. And don't keep dinner waiting; mind that now! T' rector's here, and if there's any thing that puts him about, it's waiting for his dinner."

"We asked Mr. North, father; he will be here soon."

"I'm uncommon glad you asked him. Go your ways and get your best frocks on. I'll go to t' door to meet him."

In about an hour the girls came down together, Phyllis in a pale gray satin, with delicate edgings of fine lace. It fitted her small form to perfection, close to the throat, close to the wrists, and it had about it a slight but charming touch of puritanism. There was a white japonica in her hair, and a flame-colored one at her throat, and these were her only ornaments. Elizabeth wore a plain robe of dark blue velvet, cut, as was the fashion in those days, to show the stately throat and shoulders. Splendid bracelets were on her arms, and one row of large white pearls encircled her throat. She looked like a queen, and Phyllis wished Richard could have seen her.

"She'll be a varry proper mistress o' Hallam-Croft," thought the squire, with a passing sigh. But his eyes dwelt with delight upon Phyllis. "Eh!" he said, "but thou art a bonny lass! T' flowers that bloom for thee to wear are t' happiest flowers that blow, I'll warrant thee."

After dinner the squire and his daughter went to the servants' hall to drink "loving cup" at their table, and to give their Christmas gifts. The rector, in the big chair he loved, sat smoking his long pipe. Mr. North, with a face full of the sweetest serenity and pleasure, sat opposite, his thin white hands touching each other at all their finger tips, and his clear eyes sometimes resting on the blazing fire, and sometimes drifting away to the face of Phyllis, or to that of the rector.

"You have been making people happy all day, Mr North?"

"Yes; it has been a good day to me. I had twelve pounds to give away. They made twelve homes very happy. I don't often have such a pleasure."

"I have noticed, Mr. North," said the rector, "that you do very little pastoral visiting."

"That is not my duty."

"I think it a very important part of my duty."

"You are right. It is. You are a pastor."

"And you?"

"I am a preacher. My duty is to preach Christ and him crucified. To save souls. There are others whose work it is to serve tables, and comfort and advise in trouble and perplexity."

"But you must lose all the personal and social influence of a pastor."

"If I had desired personal and social influence, I should hardly have chosen the office of a Methodist preacher. 'Out of breath pursuing souls,' was said of John Wesley and his pretorian band of helpers. I follow, as best I can, in their footsteps. But though I have no time for visiting, it is not neglected."

" Yes?" said the rector, inquiringly.

"Our class-leaders do that. John Dawson and Jacob Hargraves and Hannah Sarum are the class-leaders in Hallam and West Croft. You know them?"

" Yes."

"They are well read in the Scriptures. They have sorrowed and suffered. They understand the people. They have their local prejudices and feelings. They have been in the same straits. They speak the same tongue. It is their duty to give counsel and comfort, and material help if it is needed; to watch over young converts; to seek those that are backsliding; to use their influence in every way for such of the flock as are under their charge. John Dawson has twenty-two men and Jacob Hargraves nineteen men under their care. Hannah Sarum has a very large class. No one pastor could do as regards meat and money matters what these three can do. Besides, the wealthy, the educated, and the prosperous cannot so perfectly enter into the joys and sorrows of the poor. If a woman has a drunken husband, or a disobedient child, she will more readily go to Hannah for comfort and advice than to me; and when James Baker was out of work, it was John Dawson who loaned him five pounds, and who finally got him a job in Bowling's mill. I could have done neither of these things for him, however willing I might have been."

"I have never understood the office, then. It is a wonderful arrangement for mutual help."

"It gives to all our societies a family feeling. We are what we call ourselves—brothers and sisters;" and, with a smile, he stretched out his hand to take the one which Phyllis, by some sympathetic understanding, offered him."

"There was something like it in the apostolic Church?"

"Yes; our class-leader is the apostolic diaconate. The apostles were preachers, evangelists, hasting here and there to save souls. The deacons were the pastors of the infant churches. I preach seven times a week. I walk to all the places I preach at. It is of more importance to me that men are going to eternal destruction, than that they are needing a dinner or a coat."

"But if you settled down in one place you would soon become familiar with the people's needs; you would only have to preach two sermons a week, and you could do your own pastoral duty."

"True; but then I would not be any longer a Methodist preacher. A Methodist pastor is a solecism; Methodism is a moving evangelism. When it settles down for a life pastorate it will need a new name."

"However, Mr. North, it seems to me, that a preacher should bring every possible adjunct to aid him. The advantages of a reputation for piety, wisdom, and social sympathy are quite denied to a man who is only a preacher."

"He has the cross of Christ. It needs no aid of wealth, or wisdom, or social sympathy. It is enough for salvation. The banner of the Methodist preacher is that mighty angel flying over land and sea, and having the everlasting Gospel to preach!"

His enthusiasm had carried him away. He sighed, and continued, "But I judge no man. There must be pastors as well as preachers. I was sent to preach."

For a moment there was silence, then the fine instinct of Phyllis perceived that the conversation had reached exactly that point when it demanded relief in order to effect its best ends. She went to the piano and began to sing softly some tender little romance of home and home joys. In the midst of it the squire and Elizabeth entered, and the conversation turned upon Christmas observances. So, it fell out naturally enough that Phyllis should speak of her southern home, and describe the long rows of white cabins among the live oaks, and the kind-hearted dusky dwellers in them; and, finally, as she became almost tearful over her memories, she began to sing one of the "spirituals," then so totally unknown beyond plantation life, singing it *sotto voce*, swaying her body gently to the melody, and softly clapping her small hands as an accompaniment:

"My soul! Massa Jesus! My soul!
My soul!
Dar's a little thing lays in my heart,
An' de more I dig him, de better he spring:
My soul!
Dar's a little thing lays in my heart,
An' he set my soul on fire:
My soul!
Massa Jesus! My soul! My soul!"

Then changing the time and tune, she continued:

"De water deep, de water cold,
Nobody here to help me!
O de water rise! De water roll!
Nobody here to help me!"
Dear Lord,
Nobody here to help me!"

She had to sing them and many others over and over. Mr. North's eyes were full of tears, and the rector hid his face in his hands. As for the squire, he sat looking at her with wonder and delight.

"Why did ta nivver sing them songs afore, Phyllis? I nivver heard such music."

"It never has been written down, uncle."

"Who made it up for 'em?"

"It was never made. It sprung from their sorrows and their captivity. The slave's heart was the slave's lyre."

They talked until a deputation came from the servant's hall and asked for Mr. North. They belonged to the Christmas waits, and if he was going back to the village they wished to accompany him home; an offer he readily accepted.

"I have had a happy evening, squire;" and his smile included every one in the blessing he left behind. They all followed him to the door, and watched the little crowd take their way through the white park. The snow had quite ceased, the moon rode full and clear in mid-heaven, and near by her there was one bright, bold, steady star.

In a short time Elizabeth went with Phyllis to her room, and they laid aside their dresses and ornaments, and, sitting down before the fire, began to talk of Richard and Antony, of Rome and America, and of those innocent, happy hopes which are the joy of youth. How bright their faces were! How prettily the fire-light glinted in their white robes and loosened hair! How sweetly their low voices and rippling laughter broke the drowsy silence of the large, handsome room! Suddenly the great clock in the tower struck twelve. They counted off the strokes on their white fingers, looking into each other's faces with a bright expectancy; and after a moment's pause, out clashed the Christmas bells, answering each other from hill to hill through the moonlit midnight. Phyllis was in an ecstasy of delight. She threw open her window and stood listening, "O, I know what they say, Elizabeth. Glory be to God on high! And hark! There is singing!"

"It is the waits, Phyllis."

A company of about fifty men and women were coming through the park, filling the air as they came with music, till all the hills and valleys re-echoed the "In Excelsis Gloria" of the sweet old carol:

> "When Christ was born of Mary free,
> In Bethlehem that fair citie,
> The angels sang in holy glee,
>   'In excelsis gloria!'"

They finished the last verses under the Hall windows, and then, after a greeting from the rector and the squire, they turned happily back to the village, singing Herrick's most perfect star song:

> "Tell us, thou clear and heavenly tongue,
> Where is the Babe that lately sprung?
> Lies He the lily-banks among?"

Phyllis was weeping unrestrainedly; Elizabeth, more calm and self-contained, held her against her breast, and smiled down at the happy tears. Blessed are they who have wept for joy! They have known a rapture far beyond the power of laughter to express.

The next week was full of visiting and visitors. The squire kept open house. The butler stood at the sideboard all day long, and there was besides one large party which included all the families within a few miles of Hallam that had any acquaintance with the squire. It was, perhaps, a little trial at this time for Phyllis to explain to Elizabeth that she could not dance.

"But father is expecting to open the ball with you. He will be very much disappointed."

"I am sorry to disappoint him; but, indeed, I cannot."

"I will teach you the step and figure in half an hour."

"I do not wish to learn. I have both conscientious and womanly scruples against dancing."

"I forgot. The Methodists do not sanction dancing, I suppose; but you must admit, Phyllis, that very good people are mentioned in the Bible as dancing."

"True, Elizabeth; but the religious dances of Judea were triumphant adoration. You will hardly claim so much for the polka or waltz. All ancient dances were symbolical, and meant something. Every motion was a thought, every attitude a sentiment. If the daughter of Herodias had danced a modern cotillion, do you think that John the Baptist's head would have fallen at her feet?"

"Don't associate modern dancing with such unpleasant things. We do not want it to mean any thing but pleasure."

"But how can you find rational pleasure in spinning round like a teetotum in a room of eighty degrees temperature?"

"All people do not waltz; I do not myself."

"The square dances, then? What are they but slouching mathematical dawdling, and 'promiscuous' bobbing around?"

"But people must do something to pass the time.'

"I do not see that, Elizabeth. We are told not 'to pass the time,' but to 'redeem' it. I think dancing a foolish thing, and folly and sin are very close kin."

"You said 'unwomanly' also?"

"Yes; I think dancing is unwomanly in public. If you waltz with Lord Francis Eltham, you permit him to take a liberty with you in public you would not allow under any other circumstances. And then just look at dancers! How heated, flushed, damp, and untidy they look after the exercise! Did you ever watch a lot of men and women dancing when you could not hear the music, but could only see them bobbing up and down the room? I assure you they look just like a party of lunatics."

Elizabeth laughed; but Phyllis kept her resolution. And after the ball was over, Elizabeth said, frankly, "You had the best of it, Phyllis, every way. You looked so cool and sweet and calm in the midst of the confusion and heat. I declare every one was glad to sit down beside you, and look at you. And how cheerfully you sang and played! You did not dance, but, nevertheless, you were the belle of the ball."

On the first Sabbath of the new year Phyllis was left at the little Methodist chapel. Her profession had always been free from that obtrusive demonstration of religious opinion which is seldom united with true piety. While she dwelt under her uncle's roof it had seemed generally the wisest and kindest thing to worship with his family. It involved nothing that hurt her conscience, and it prevented many disputes which would probably have begun in some small household disarrangement, and bred only dislike and religious offense. Her Methodism had neither been cowardly nor demonstrative, but had been made most conscious to all by her sweet complaisance and charitable concessions.

So, when she said to the squire, "Uncle, Mr. North tells me there is to be a very solemn Methodist service to-morrow, and one which I never saw in America; I should like you to leave me at the chapel," he answered: "To be sure, Phyllis. We would go with thee, but there's none but members admitted. I know what service thou means well enough."

She found in the chapel about two hundred men and women, for they had come to Hallam from the smaller societies around. They were mostly from what is often called "the lower orders," men and women whose hands were hard with toil, and whose forms were bowed with labor. But what a still solemnity there was in the place! No organ, no dim religious light, no vergers, or beadles, or robed choristers, or priest in sacred vestments. The winter light fell pale and cold through the plain windows on bare white-washed walls, on a raised wooden pulpit, and on pews unpainted and uncushioned. Some of the congregation were very old; some, just in the flush of manhood and womanhood. All were in the *immediate* presence of God, and were intensely conscious of it.

There was a solemn hymn sung and a short prayer; then Mr. North's gaze wandered over the congregation until it rested upon a man in the center—a very old man—with hair as white as wool.

"Stephen Langside, can you stand up before God and man to-day?"

The old man rose, and, supported by two young farmers, lifted up a face full of light and confidence.

"They tell me that you are ninety-eight years old, and that this is the seventy-first time that you will renew your covenant with the eternal Father. Bear witness this day of him."

"His word is sure as t' everlasting hills! I hev been young, and now I'm old, and I hev hed a deal to do wi' him, and he hes hed a deal to do for me; and he nivver hes deceived me, and he hes nivver failed me, and he has nivver turned t' cold shoulder to me; ay, and he hes stuck up to his promises, when I was none ready to keep mine. There's many good masters, but he is t' best Master of a'! There's many true friends, but he is the truest of a'! Many a kind father, but no father so kind as him! I *know* whom I hev believed, and I can trust him even unto death!"

"Brothers and sisters, this is the Master, the Friend, the Father, whom I ask you to enter into covenant with to-day—a holy solemn covenant, which you shall kneel down and make upon your knees, and stand up and ratify in the sight of angels and of men."

Not ignorantly did Phyllis enter into this covenant with her Maker. She had read it carefully over, and considered well its awful solemnity. Slowly the grand abnegation, the solemn engagement, was formed; every sentence recited without haste, and with full consciousness of all its obligations. Then Mr. North, after a short pause for mental examination, said:

"Remember now that you are in the actual presence of the Almighty God. He is nearer to you than breathing, closer than hands and feet. He besets you before and behind. He lays his hand upon you. Therefore let all who, by standing up, give their soul's assent to this consecration, remember well to whom they promise."

Slowly, one by one, the congregation arose; and so they remained standing, until every face was lifted. Then the silence was broken by the joyful singing of Doddridge's fine hymn,

"O happy day that fixed my choice,"

and the service closed with the administration of the Holy Communion.

"Thou looks very happy, Phyllis," said the squire to her, as they both sat by the fire that night.

"I am very happy, uncle."

"Thou beats me! I told t' rector where ta had gone to-day, and he said it were a varry singular thing that thou should take such an obligation on thee. He said t' terms of it would do for t' varry strictest o' Roman Catholic orders."

"Do you not think, uncle, that Protestants should be as strict regarding personal holiness as Catholics?"

"Nay, I know nowt about it, dearie. I wish women were a' like thee, though. They'd be a deal better to live wi'. I like religion in a woman, it's a varry reliable thing. I wish Antony hed hed his senses about him, and got thee to wed him. Eh! but I would have been a happy father!"

"Uncle, dear—you see—I love somebody else."

"Well I nivver! Thee! Why thou's too young! When did ta begin to think o' loving any body?"

"When I was a little girl John Millard and I loved each other. I don't know when I began to love him, I always loved him."

"What is ta talking about? Such nonsense!"

"Love is not nonsense, uncle. You remember the old English song you like so much:

"'O 'tis love, 'tis love, 'tis love
That makes the world go round!'"

"Now be quiet wi' thee. It's nowt o' t' sort. Songs and real life are varry different things. If ta comes to real life, it's money, and not love; t' world would varry soon stick without a bit o' money."

About the middle of January Richard returned to Hallam. The Bishop was with friends in Liverpool, but he wished to sail immediately, and Richard thought it best to sail with him. Phyllis was willing to go. She had had a charming visit, but she had many duties and friends on the other side, and her heart, also, was there. As for danger or discomfort in a winter passage, she did not think it worth consideration. Some discomfort there must be; and if storm, or even death came, she was as near to heaven by sea as by land.

The squire had not written to Richard about his plans for the succession of Hallam. He had felt more uncertainty on the subject than he would admit even to his own heart. He thought he would prefer to explain matters to him in person. So, one morning, as they were together, he said "Look 'ee here, Richard!" and he led him to the portrait of Colonel Alfred Hallam. "Thou can see where ta comes from. Thou is t' varry marrow o' that Hallam!"

Richard was much pleased at the incident, and he traced with pleasure the resemblances between them.

"Richard, I am going to leave Hallam to thee."

It was not in the squire's nature to "introduce" a subject. He could never half say a thing. His bald statement made Richard look curiously at him. He never for a moment believed him to mean what the words implied. So he only smiled and bowed.

"Nay, thou needn't laugh! It's no laughing matter. I'll tell thee all about it."

In the squire's way of telling, the tale was a very short one. The facts were stated in a few sentences, without comment. They amazed Richard, and left him for a moment speechless.

"Well, what does ta say?"

"I will be as frank as you have been, uncle. I cannot possibly accept your offer."

"Thou'lt hev a reason?"

"More than one. First, I would not change my name. I should feel as if I had slandered the Fontaines. My father was a brave soldier; my grandfather was a missionary, whose praise is in all our churches. I need go no farther back. If I had been born 'Hallam' I would have stood by the name just as firmly."

"Then, thou wilt hev to give up Elizabeth. Succession must go in her children and in her name."

"Miss Hallam and you accepted me as Richard Fontaine. Have I not the right to expect that both she and you will keep your word with me?"

"Thou forgets, Richard. Her duty to her father and to her ancestors stands before thee. If thy duty to thine will not let thee give up thy name, hers may well be due to home and lands that hold her by a tenure o' a thousand years. But neither Miss Hallam nor Hallam Hall need go a-begging, lad. I ask thy pardon for offering thee owt so worthless."

"Dear uncle, do not be angry with me."

"Ay, ay; it's 'dear uncle,' and 'dear father,' but

it's also, 'I'll tak' my own way', wi' both Antony and thee. I'm a varry unhappy old man. I am that!"

He walked angrily off, leaving Richard standing before the picture which so much resembled him. He turned quickly, and went in search of Elizabeth. She was sitting with Phyllis in the breakfast parlor. Phyllis, who was often inclined to a dreamy thoughtfulness, was so inclined at that hour, and she was answering Elizabeth's remarks, far more curious of some mental vision than of the calm-browed woman, sitting opposite to her, sewing so industriously. Richard came in like a small tempest, and for once Elizabeth's quiet, inquiring regard seemed to irritate him.

"Elizabeth;" and he took her work from her hand, and laid it on the table. "My dear love! does Phyllis know?"

"What, Richard?"

"About Antony and the Hallam estate?"

"No; I thought it best to let you tell her."

"Because you were sure I would refuse it?—Phyllis!"

"Yes, Richard."

"Your uncle is going to disinherit Antony; and he wishes me to become his heir and take his name."

"But that is impossible. You could not take Antony's place. You could not give up your name —not for a kingdom."

"Then," said Elizabeth, a little proudly, "he must give me up. I cannot disobey my father."

Phyllis quietly rose and went out. She could not interfere with the lovers, but she felt sorry enough for them. Richard's compliance was forbidden by every sentiment of honor. Elizabeth was little likely to give way. Richard held her to her promise, and pleaded for its fulfillment. He wanted no fortune. He was quite content that her fortune should go to free Hallam. But he did not see that her life and happiness, and his, also, should be sacrificed to Antony's insane ambition. "He will marry, doubtless," he urged. "He may have a large family; cannot one of them, in such case, be selected as heir?"

This was the only hope Elizabeth would admit. In her way she was as immovable as Richard. She had made up her mind as to what was her duty in the premises, and her lover could not move her from this position. And, as the unhappy can seldom persuade themselves that "sufficient unto the day is the evil thereof," each heart was heavy with the probable sorrows that were to flow from this complication of affairs.

Phyllis, musing thoughtfully at her own room window, saw the squire walking on the terrace. Her first impulse was to go to him, but she sat down to consider the inclination. Her class-leader, a shrewd, pious old Scotchman, had once said to her—"Nine impulses oot o' ten, Sister Phyllis, come fra the de'il

Just put an impulse through its catechism before ye go the gate it sends ye." So she sat down to think. " What right have I to interfere? Ought I to solicit a confidence? Can I do good? Might I not do harm? A good word spoken out of season is often a bad word; and I am not sure what is the good word in this case. I had better be still and wait."

Her patience had in some measure its reward. Toward afternoon Elizabeth came to her room. Her eyes were red with weeping, but she said, " Father and Richard have shaken hands, Phyllis; there is to be no ill-will about the disappointment."

" I am very glad. But is it to be a disappointment—to you, I mean, Elizabeth ? "

" I fear so; I must stand by father's side as regards Hallam. I can wait and love on. But I will not bind Richard. He is free."

" I am quite sure he is not free. Richard will never be free while there remains a hope of eventually winning you."

" He says that nothing but my marriage to some other person shall make him lose hope; but men say these things and forget."

" Richard means what he says. He will not forget; and time gives with both hands to the patient and the truthful. Is the squire satisfied ? "

" I don't think he blames Richard. The shadow I felt on the night of our betrothal has begun to creep toward me, Phyllis. I am in its chill and gloom. It will darken all our remaining hours together, and they are few now."

"Make the most of them, dear. Get all the sunshine you can; stay with Richard. I am going to the village to bid Martha good-bye."

"Richard says you are to sail Wednesday?"

"Yes; what is the use of drawing out a parting? We have had a happy holiday. Let us go ere its spirit is over. There must be times and seasons, Elizabeth; it is the part of love and wisdom never to force them. Besides, uncle has a very sore place in his heart, and Richard can hardly avoid rubbing against it. It is best for us to go."

Martha was a little dull, and Phyllis was struck with her explanation: "I'm a bit selfish to-day; and t' heart that isn't loving isn't cheerful. Ben and me hev been so much to each other, that it comes a bit hard to hev to step aside for a lass as one doesn't care much for." She put her checked apron to her eyes, and wiped away a few tears.

"But Ben can never forget what you did for him."

"It was Mary after a' that saved him. I nobbut prayed night and day. She brought the magistrate and t' constable. Men don't count much on prayer."

"Dear Martha, God sends by whom he will send. If he had thought it best, you would have got the order. God looks afar off—for the years that are to come—when you may be where all tears are wiped away."

"I know, I know."

"Don't let Ben think you grudge him the fullest measure of his happiness and deliverance. Mothers must have a deal to bear. The best of children are blind, I think."

Martha was crying quietly. "He was t' last left me. I hev carried him i' my heart for months, till my heart is fair empty without him. I wanted him a little bit to mysen. She's a good girl, is Mary, and I'm trying hard to love her; but I've got a weight on me that's bad to bide."

"If it's a bitter cup, drink it, Martha."

"My lass, I'll do that. There'll be a blessing in t' bottom o' it, never fear. I'm nobbut standing as a bairn does wi' a cup o' medicine; and when a thing is hard to take, its nobbut human nature to say it's none nice."

"I am come to say 'good-bye,' Martha; I don't want to leave you in tears."

"Nay, then, is ta! Surely to goodness thou isn't going in t' dead o' winter?"

"Yes. We leave Hallam to-morrow."

"Then bide a bit. I'll mak' a cup o' tea in t' little Wesley tea-pot; and I'll toast thee a Yorkshire cake, and we'll eat a mouthful together in this world before we part. We'll be none like to meet again."

She wiped away every trace of tears, and drew the little table to the hearth-stone, and set out her humble service. And she quite put away her own trouble and spoke cheerfully, and served Phyllis with busy hospitality.

"For, you see," she said, as she knelt before the fire toasting the cake, "I feel as if you were a pilgrim, Sister Phyllis, that had come across my little cottage on your way to the kingdom. And if I didn't mak' you welcome, and say a hearty, loving 'Godspeed' to you, I'd happen miss a bit o' my own welcome when I enter the gates o' the kingdom. So, eat and drink, dearie; and may the bread strengthen you, and the cup be full o' blessing."

"I shall never forget you, Martha. I think we shall know each other when we meet again."

"For sure we will. It will be in 'Jerusalem the golden' I don't doubt. Farewell, sister!" and she took the sweet young face between her large hands and kissed it.

Her smile was bright, her words cheerful, but Phyllis went down the street with a heavy heart. She stopped at the house where Mr. North lodged and asked to see him. He came down to her with a smile; but when she said, "It is a good-bye, Mr. North," his face grew pale, his eyes full of trouble; he was unable to answer her. The silence became painful, and Phyllis rose.

"Let me walk a little way with you. Pardon me, I was not prepared for this—blow."

Then Phyllis knew that he loved her. Then he knew it himself. A great pity was in her heart. She was silent and constrained, and they walked together as two who are walking toward a grave.

"It is very hard for me to say 'good-bye,' Miss Fontaine. I shall never, never forget you."

"There are many hard things in life, Mr. North; we can but bear them."

"Is that all?"

"That is all."

"God help me!" He lifted her gloved hand and touched it with his lips. No knight could have expressed in the act more respect, more hopeless tenderness. Then he turned silently away. Phyllis's lips parted, but no words would come. She was full of sorrow for the noble, suffering, humble heart. She longed to say a kind word, and yet felt that it would be unkind; and she stood still watching him as he went farther and farther away. At a bend in the road he turned and saw her standing. The level rays of the sun set her in a clear amber light. He gazed at her steadily for a moment, raised his hand slowly, and passed forever from her sight.

There was something so pathetic and yet so lofty in the slight, vanishing figure, with the hand lifted heavenward, that she felt strangely affected, and could scarcely restrain her tears.

When people come to the end of a pleasure, so many little things show it. The first enthusiasms are gone, there is a little weariness in joy, the heart begins to turn to those fundamental affections and those homely ties which are the main reliance of life. It seemed to Phyllis that, for the first time, she was homesick. The low, white, rambling wooden house, spreading itself under moss-covered trees, began to grow very fair in her memory. The mocking-birds were calling her across the sea. She remembered the tangles of the yellow jasmine, the merry darkies chatting and singing and laughing, and her soul turned westward with an indescribable longing.

And she thought to herself, as she stood upon the terrace and looked over the fair land she was leaving with so little regret, "When the time comes for me to go to my heavenly home, I shall be just as willing to leave the earthly one."

CHAPTER V.

"I loved you alway, I will not deny it; not for three months, and not for a year; but I loved you from the first, when I was a child, and my love shall not wither, till death shall end me."—GAELIC SONG.

"Our own acts are our attending angels, in whose light or shadow we walk continually."

THE Fontaine place was a long, low, white building facing a tumbling sea, and a stretch of burnt sea-sands. It had no architectural beauty, and yet it was a wonderfully picturesque place. Broad piazzas draped in vines ran all around the lower story, and the upper revealed itself only in white glimpses among dense masses of foliage. And what did it matter that outside the place there were brown sand-hills and pale-sailed ships? A high hedge of myrtles hid it in a large garden full of the scents of the sun-burnt South—a garden of fragrant beauty, where one might dream idly all day long.

It was four o'clock in the afternoon of an August day, and every thing was still; only the *cicadas* ran from hedge to hedge telling each other, in clear resonant voices, how hot it was. The house door stood open, but all the green jalousies were closed, and not a breath of air stirred the lace curtains hanging motionless before the windows. The rooms, large and lofty, were in a dusky light, their atmosphere still and warm and heavy with the scent of flowers. On the back piazza half a dozen negro children were sleeping in all sorts of picturesque attitudes, a bright mulatto women was dozing in a rocking-chair, and the cook, having "fixed" his dinner ready for the stove, had rolled himself in his blanket on the kitchen floor. Silence and dusk were every-where, the dwelling might have been an enchanted one, and life in it held in a trance.

In one of the upper rooms there was an occupant well calculated to carry out this idea. It was Phyllis, fast asleep upon a white couch, with both hands dropped toward the floor. But the sewing which had fallen from them, and the thimble still upon her finger, was guarantee for her mortality. And in a few minutes she opened her soft, dark eyes, and smiled at her vacant hands. Then she glanced at the windows; the curtains were beginning to stir, the gulf breeze had sprung up, the birds were twittering, and the house awakening.

But it was pleasant to be quiet and think in such an indolent mood; and Phyllis had some reasons for finding the "thinking" engrossing. First, she had had a letter from Elizabeth, and it was in a very hopeful tone. Antony and George Eltham were doing very well, and, as Lord Eltham had become quietly interested in the firm, the squire felt more easy as to its final success. Second, Mr. North was leaving Hallam, his term there had expired, and the Conference, which would determine his next movement, was then sitting. Her thoughts were drifting on these two topics when a woman softly entered the room. She looked at Phyllis's closed eyes, and with a smile went here and there laying out clean white muslins, and knots of pink ribbons, and all the pretty accessories of a young maiden's evening toilet.

"Thar now, Miss Phill! I'se ready—and I 'spects thar's some good news for you, honey!"

Phyllis opened her eyes. "I heard you, Harriet. I was not asleep. As for good news, I think you are always expecting it—besides, I had some to-day."

"Dat's de reason, Miss Phill—'whar you going good news? Jest whar I'se been afore.' Dat's de way. I reckon I knows 'bout it."

"What makes you know this time, Harriet? Has the postman been, or a bird whispered it to you, or have some of Waul's servants been making a call here?"

"I don't 'ceive any of de Waul's servants, Miss Phill. I'se not wanting my char'ctar hung on ebery tree top in de county. No, I draws my s'picions in de properest way. Mass'r Richard git a letter dis morning. Did he tell you, Miss Phill?"

"I have not seen him since breakfast."

"I thought he'd kind ob hold back 'bout dat letter. I knows dat letter from Mass'r John. I'se sure ob it."

"Did you look—at the outside of it, I mean—Harriet?"

"No, Miss Phill, I didn't look neider at de outside, nor de inside; I's not dat kind; I look at Mass'r Richard's face. Bless you, Miss Phill! Mass'r Richard kaint hide nothing. If he was in love Harriet would know it, quick as a flash—"

"I think not, Harriet."

"Den I tell you something, Miss Phill. Mass'r Richard been in love eber since he come back from ober de Atterlantic Ocean. P'raps you don't know, but I done found him out."

Phyllis laughed.

"I tell you how I knows it. Mass'r Richard allays on de lookout for de postman; and he gits a heap ob dem bluish letters wid a lady's face in de corner."

"That is Queen Victoria's face. You don't suppose Master Richard is in love with Queen Victoria?"

"Miss Phill, de Fontaines would fall in love wid de moon, and think dey pay her a compliment—dey mighty proud fambly, de Fontaines; but I'se no such fool as not to know de lady's head am worth so many cents to carry de letter. But, Miss Phill, who sends de letters? Dat am de question."

"Of course, that would decide it."

"Den when Mass'r Richard gits one of dem letters, he sits so quiet-like, thinking and smiling to himself, and ef you speak to him, he answers you kind ob far-away, and gentle. I done tried him often. But he didn't look like dat at all when he git de letter dis morning. Mass'r Richard got powerful high temper, Miss Phill."

"Then take care and not anger him, Harriet."

"You see, when I bring in de letter, I bring in wid me some fresh myrtles and de tube roses for de vases, and as I put dem in, and fixed up de chimley-piece, I noticed Mass'r Richard through de looking-glass—and he bit his lips, and he drew his brows together, and he crush'd de letter up in his hand."

"Harriet, you have no right to watch your master. It is a very mean thing to do."

"Me watch Mass'r Richard! Now, Miss Phill, I'se none ob dat kind! But I kaint shut my eyes, 'specially when I'se 'tending to de flower vases."

"You could have left the vases just at that time."

"No, Miss Phill, I'se very partic'lar 'bout de vases. Dey has to be 'tended to. You done told me ober and ober to hab a time for ebery thing, and de time for de vases was jist den."

"Then, the next time you see Master Richard through the glass, tell him so, Harriet; that is only fair, you know."

"Go 'way, Miss Phill! I'se got more sense dan tell Mass'r Richard any sich thing."

Phyllis did not answer; she was thinking of a decision she might be compelled to make, and the question was one which touched her very nearly on very opposite sides. She loved her brother with all her heart. Their lives had been spent together, for Phyllis had been left to his guardianship when very young, and had learned to give him an affection which had something in it of the clinging reliance of the child, as well as of the proud regard of the sister. But John Millard she loved, as women love but once. He was related by marriage to the Fontaines, and had, when Phyllis and Richard were children, spent much of his time at the Fontaine place.

But even as boys Richard and John had not agreed. To ask "why" is to ask a question which in such cases is never fully answered. It is easy to say that Richard was jealous of his sister, and jealous of John's superiority in athletic games, and that John spoke sneeringly of Richard's aristocratic airs, and finer gentleman ways; but there was something deeper than these things, a natural antipathy, for which there seemed to be no reason, and for which there was no cure but the compelling power of a divine love.

John Millard had been for two years on the frontier, and there had been very meager and irregular news from him. If any one had asked Richard, "Are you really hoping that he has been killed in some Indian fight?" Richard would have indignantly denied it; and yet he knew that if such a fate had come to his cousin Millard, he would not have been sorry.

And now the man, with the easy confidence of a soldier who is accustomed to make his own welcome, wrote to say "that he was coming to New Orleans, and hoped to spend a good deal of his time with them."

The information was most unwelcome to Richard. He was not anxious for his sister to marry; least of all, to marry a frontier settler. He could not endure the thought of Phyllis roughing life in some log-cabin on the San Marino. That was at least the aspect in which he put the question to himself. He meant that he could not endure that John Millard should at the last get the better of him about his own sister. And when he put his foot down passionately, and said, between his closed teeth, "He shall not do it!" it was the latter thought he answered.

He felt half angry at Phyllis for being so lovely when she sat down opposite him at dinner time. And there was an unusual light in her eyes and an indescribable elation in her manner which betrayed her knowledge of the coming event to him.

"Phyllis," he asked, suddenly, "who told you John Millard was coming?"

"Harriet told me you had a letter from him this morning."

"Confound—"

"Richard!"

"I beg your pardon, Phyllis. Be so good as to keep Harriet out of my way. Yes; I had a letter—

a most impertinent one, I think. Civilized human beings usually wait for an invitation."

"Unless they imagine themselves going to a home."

"Home?"

"Yes. I think this is, in some sense, John's home. Mother always made him welcome to it. Dear Richard, if it is foolish to meet troubles, it is far more foolish to meet quarrels."

"I do not wish to quarrel, Phyllis; if John does not talk to you as he ought not to talk. He ought to have more modesty than to ask you to share such a home as he can offer you."

"Richard, dear, you are in a bad way. There is a trustees' meeting to-night, and they are in trouble about dollars and cents; I would go, if I were you."

"And have to help the deficiency?"

"Yes; when a man has been feeling unkindly, and talking unkindly, the best of all atonements is to do a good deed."

"O, Phyllis! Phyllis!"

"Yes, Richard; and you will see the Bishop there, very likely; and you can tell the good old man what is in your heart, and I know what he will say. 'It is but fair and square, son Richard, to treat a man kindly till he does you some wrong which deserves unkindness.' He will say, 'Son Richard, if you have not the proofs upon which to blame a man, don't blame him upon likelihoods.'"

"My good little sister, what do you want me to do?"

"I want you to meet John, as we were met at Hallam, with trusting courtesy."

"If you will promise me to—"

"I will promise you to do nothing secretly; to do nothing my mother would blame me for. To ask more, is to doubt me, and doubt I do not deserve. Now put on your hat and go to church. They will be disappointed if you are absent."

"It will cost me $100."

"A man ought to pay his debts; and it is nicer to go and pay them than to compel some one to call here and ask you to do it."

"A debt?"

"Call it a gift, if you like. When I look over the cotton-fields, Richard, and see what a grand crop you are going to have this year, somehow I feel as if you ought to have said $200."

"Give me my hat, Phyllis. You have won, as you always do." And he stooped and kissed her, and then went slowly through the garden to the road.

She did not see him again that night, but in the morning he was very bright and cheerful. "I am going to ride to Greyson's Timbers, Phyllis," he said; "I have some business with Greyson, and John will be almost sure to 'noon' there. So we shall likely come back together."

She smiled gladly, but knew her brother too well to either inquire into his motives or comment upon them. It was sufficient that Richard had conquered his lower self, and whether the victory had been a single-handed one, or whether the Bishop had been an ally, was not of vital importance. One may enjoy the perfume of a good action without investigating the processes of its production.

In the middle of the afternoon she heard their arrival. It was a pleasant thing to hear the sound of men's voices and laughter, and all that cheerful confusion which as surely follows their advent as thunder follows lightning. And Phyllis found it very pleasant to lie still and think of the past, and put off, just for an hour or two, whatever of joy or sorrow was coming to meet her; for she had not seen John for two years. He might have ceased to love her. He might be so changed that she would not dare to love him. But in the main she thought hopefully. True love, like true faith, when there seems to be nothing at all to rest upon,

"Treads on the void and finds
The rock beneath."

Few women will blame Phyllis for being unusually careful about her toilet, and for going down stairs with a little tremor at her heart. Even when she could hear Richard and John talking, she still delayed the moment she had been longing for. She walked into the dining-room, looked at the boy setting the table, and altered the arrangement of the flowers. She looked into the parlor, raised a curtain, and opened the piano, and then, half ashamed of her self-consciousness, went to the front piazza, where the young men were sitting.

There was a subtle likeness between Richard and his English ancestors that neither intermarriage, climate, nor educational surroundings had been able to overcome; but between him and John Millard there were radical dissimilarities. Richard was sitting on the topmost of the broad white steps which led from the piazza to the garden. With the exception of a narrow black ribbon round his throat, he was altogether dressed in white; and this dress was a singularly becoming contrast to his black hair and glowing dark eyes. And in every attitude which he took he managed his tall stature with an indolent grace suggestive of an unlimited capacity for pride, passion, aristocratic—or cottonocratic—self-sufficiency. In his best moods he was well aware of the dangerous points in his character, and kept a guard over them; otherwise they came prominently forward; and, sitting in John Millard's presence, Richard Fontaine was very much indeed the Richard Fontaine of a nature distinctly overbearing and uncontrolled.

John Millard leaned against the pillar of the piazza, talking to him. He had a brown, handsome face, and short, brown, curly hair. His eyes were very large and blue, with that steely look in them which snaps like lightning when any thing strikes fire from the heart. He was very tall and straight, and had a lofty carriage and an air of command. His dress was that of an ordinary frontiersman, and he wore no arms of any kind, yet any one would have said, with the invincible assurance of a sudden presentiment, "The man is a soldier."

Richard and he were talking of frontier defense, and Richard, out of pure contradiction, was opposing it. In belittling the cause he had some idea that he was snubbing the man who had been fighting for it. John was just going to reply when Phyllis's approach broke the sentence in two, and he did not finish it. He stood still watching her, his whole soul in his face; and, when he took her hands, said, heartily, "O, Phyllis, I am so happy to see you again! I was afraid I never would!"

"What nonsense!" said Richard, coldly: "a journey to Europe is a trifle—no need to make a fuss about it; is there, Phyllis? Come, let us go to dinner. I hear the bell."

Before dinner was over the sun had set and the moon risen. The mocking-birds were singing, the fire-flies executing, in the sweet, languid atmosphere, a dance full of mystery. The garden was like a land of enchantment. It was easy to sit still and let the beauty of heaven and earth sink into the heart. And for some time John was contented with it. It was enough to sit and watch the white-robed figure of Phyllis, which was thrown into the fairest relief by the green vines behind it. And Richard was silent because he was trying to conquer his resentment at

John finding satisfaction in the exquisite picture. Perhaps few people understand how jealous a true brotherly love can be, how tenderly careful of a sister's welfare, how watchful of all that pertains to her future happiness, how proud of her beauty and her goodness, how exacting of all pretenders to her favor. His ideal husband for Phyllis was not John Millard. He wondered what she could see to admire in the bronzed frontier soldier. He wondered how John could dare to think of transplanting a gentlewoman like Phyllis from the repose and luxury of her present home to the change and dangers and hardships of pioneer life.

It would have been an uncomfortable evening if the Bishop had not called. He looked at John and loved him. Their souls touched each other when they clasped hands. Perhaps it was because the nature of both men was militant—perhaps because both men loved frontier fighting. "I like," said the old soldier of Christ, " I dearly like to follow the devil to his outposts. He has often fine fellows in them, souls well worth saving. I was the first Methodist—I may say the first Protestant preacher—that entered Washington County, in Texas. Texas was one of our mission stations in 1837. I never was as happy as when lifting the cross of Christ in some camp of outlaws."

" Did they listen to you ?"

" Gladly. Many of them clung to it. The worst of them respected and protected me. One night I came to a lonely log-house in the Brazos woods—that was 'far, far West' then. I think the eight men in it were thieves; I believe that they intended to rob, and perhaps to murder, me. But they gave me supper, and took my saddle-bags, and put up my horse. 'Reckon you're from the States,' one said. 'Twelve months ago.' 'Any news?' 'The grandest. If you'll get your boys together I'll tell you it.'"

They gathered very quickly, lit their pipes, and sat down; and, sitting there among them, I preached the very best sermon I ever preached in my life. I was weeping before I'd done, and they were just as wretched as I like to see sinners. I laid down among them and slept soundly and safely. Ten years afterward I gave the sacrament to four of these very men in Bastrop Methodist Church. If I was a young man I would be in the Rio Grande District. I would carry 'the glad tidings' to the ranger camps on the Chicon and the Secor, and the United States forts on the Mexican border. It is 'the few sheep in the wilderness' that I love to seek; yea, it is the scape-goats that, loaded with the sins of civilized communities, have been driven from among them!"

Richard started to his feet. "My dear father, almost you persuade me to be a missionary!"

"Ah, son Richard, if you had the 'call' it would be no uncertain one! You would not say 'almost;' but it is a grand thing to feel your heart stir to the trumpet, even though you don't buckle on the armor.

A respectable, cold indifference makes me despair of a soul. I have more hope for a flagrant sinner."

"I am sure," said John, "our camp on the San Saba would welcome you. One night a stranger came along who had with him a child—a little chap about five years old. He had been left an orphan, and the man was taking him to an uncle that lived farther on. As we were sitting about the fire he said, 'I'm going into the wagon now. I'm going to sleep. Who'll hear my prayers?' And half a dozen of the boys said, 'I will,' and he knelt down at the knee of Bill Burleson, and clasped his hands and said 'Our Father;' and I tell you, sir, there wasn't a dry eye in camp when the little chap said 'Amen.' And I don't believe there was an oath or a bad word said that night; every one felt as if there was an angel among us."

"Thank you, John Millard. I like to hear such incidents. It's hard to kill the divinity in any man. And you are on the San Saba? Tell me about it."

It was impossible for Richard to resist the enthusiasm of the conversation which followed. He forgot all his jealousy and pride, and listened, with flashing eyes and eager face, and felt no angry impulse, although Phyllis sat between the Bishop and John, and John held her hand in his. But when the two young men were left alone the reaction came to Richard. He was shy and cold. John did not perceive it; he was too happy in his own thoughts.

"What a tender heart your sister has, Richard. Did you see how interested she was when I was telling about the sufferings of the women and children on the frontier?"

"No; I fancied she was rather bored."

John was at once dashed, and looked into Richard's face, and felt as if he had been making a bragging fool of himself. And Richard was angry, and ashamed, for a gentleman never tells a lie, though it be only to his own consciousness, without feeling unspeakably mean. And by a reflex motion of accountability he was angry with John for provoking him into so contemptible a position.

The "good-night" was a cooler one than the evening had promised; but Richard had recollected himself before he met John in the morning; and John, for Phyllis's sake, was anxious to preserve a kindly feeling. Love made him wise and forbearing; and he was happy, and happiness makes good men tolerant; so that Richard soon saw that John would give him no excuse for a quarrel. He hardly knew whether he was glad or sorry, and the actions and speech of one hour frequently contradicted those of the next.

Still there followed many days of sunshine and happy leisure, of boating and fishing, of riding upon the long stretch of hard sands, of sweet, silent games of chess in shady corners, of happy communion in song and story, and of conscious conversations wherein so few words meant so much. And perhaps the lovers in their personal joy grew a little selfish, for one night the Bishop said to Phyllis, "Come and see me in the morning, daughter, I have something to say to you."

He was sitting waiting for her under an enormous fig-tree, a tree so large that the space it shadowed made a pretty parlor, with roof and walls of foliage so dense that not even a tropical shower could penetrate them. He sat in a large wicker-chair, and on the rustic table beside him was a cup of coffee, a couple of flaky biscuits, and a plate of great purple figs, just gathered from the branches above him. When Phyllis came, he pulled a rocking-chair to his side, and touched a little hand-bell. "You shall have some coffee with me, and some bread and fruit; eating lubricates talking, dear, and I want to talk to you —very seriously."

"About John, father?"

"Yes, about John. You know your own mind, Phyllis Fontaine? You are not playing with a good man's heart?"

"I told you two years ago, father, that I loved John. I love him still. I have applied the test my leader gave me, and which I told you of. I am more than willing to take John for eternity; I should be miserable if I thought death could part us."

"Very good—so far; that is, for John and yourself. But you must think of Richard. He has claims upon you, also. Last night I saw how he suffered, how he struggled to subdue his temper. Phyllis, any moment that temper may subdue him, and then there will be sorow. You must come to some understanding with him. John and you may enjoy the romance of your present position, and put off, with the unreasonable selfishness of lovers, matter-of-fact details, but Richard has a right to them."

"Am I selfish, father?"

"I think you are."

"What must I do?"

"Send John to speak plainly to Richard. That will give your brother an opportunity to say what he wishes. If the young men are not likely to agree, tell John to propose my advice in the matter. You can trust me to do right, daughter?"

"Yes, I can."

In the evening Phyllis called on the Bishop again. He was walking in his garden enjoying the cool breeze, and when he saw her carriage he went to meet her. A glance into her face was sufficient. He led her into the little parlor under the fig-tree. "So you are in trouble, Phyllis?"

"Yes, father. The conversation you advised had unfortunately, taken place before I got an opportunity to speak to John. There has been a quarrel."

"What was said?"

"I scarcely know how the conversation began; but Richard told John, that people were talking about his intimacy with me; and that, as marriage was impossible between us, the intimacy must cease."

"What else?"

"I do not know; many hard things were said on both sides, and John went away in a passion."

"Go home and see your brother, and make some concessions to his claim upon your love. Tell him that you will not marry John for two years; that will give John time to prepare in some measure for your comfort. Promise in addition any thing that is reasonable. I fear Richard's temper, but I fear John's more; for the anger of a patient man is a deep anger, and John has been patient, very. Don't you be impatient, Phyllis. Wait for time to carry you over the stream, and don't fling yourself into the flood, and perish."

"Two years!"

"But reflect—a quarrel becomes a duel here very readily—dare you provoke such a possibility?"

"Dear father, pray for me."

"I will. Trust God, and every rod shall blossom for you. Be patient and prudent. Birds build their nests before they mate, and love needs the consecration of a home. Tell John to make one for you, and then to come and speak to Richard again. I don't say, wait for riches; but I do say, wait for comforts. Comforts keep men innocent, bind them to virtue by the strong cords of friends, families, homes, and the kindnesses of kindred."

But when Phyllis arrived at home Richard was not there. He had gone to the plantation, and left word for his sister that he might not return until late the following day. Phyllis was very wretched. She could hardly trust the message. It was possible that Richard had considered flight from temptation the wisest course, and that he expected John would leave during his absence. On the other hand, it was just as likely that John would not leave, and that the quarrel would be renewed at the hotel, or upon the street, under circumstances where every influence would be against the young men.

She was sure that if she had John's promise to keep peace with Richard, that he would not break it; but she did not know whether he was still in the village or had gone away altogether. If the latter, she would certainly receive some message from him; and, if no message came, she must conclude that he was waiting for an opportunity to see her.

Harriet was sure that he was at the village 'hotel.' "Dime done seen him thar," she said, positively, "and Mass'r John no sich fool as go 'way widout talkin' up for himself. I was 'stonished dis afternoon, Miss Phill, he took Mass'r Richard's worryin' dat quiet-like; but I could see de bearin's ob things mighty plain."

"You heard the quarrel, then, Harriet?"

"Couldn't help hearin' ob it, Miss Phill, no way; 'case I right thar. I was in de dinin'-room fixin' up de clean window curtains, and de young gen'lemen were on de p'azza. Cassie never do fix de curtains right; she's not got de hang ob dem, Miss Phill; so I jist made up my mind to do 'em myself; and while I was busy as a honey-bee 'bout dem, Mass'r Richard he walk proud-like up to Mass'r John, and say, ' he want to speak a few words wid him.' Den I kind ob open my ears, case, Miss Phill, when gen'lemen want to ' say a few words,' dey're most ob de time onpleasant ones."

" Did Master John answer ? "

" He looked kind ob ' up-head,' and says he, ' Dat all right. I'se nothin' 'gainst you sayin' dem.' So Mass'r Richard he tell him dat he hear some talk down town, and dat he won't have you talked 'bout, and dat as thar was to be no marryin' 'tween you two, Mass'r John better go 'way."

" Did Master Richard say ' go away,' Harriet ? "

" Dat's jist what he say—' go 'way,' and Mass'r John he flash up like, and say, he sorry to be turn'd out ob de ole home, and dat he'll go as soon as he see you. Den Mass'r Richard, he git up in one ob his white-hot still tempers, and he say, ' No gen'lemen need more 'an one word ; ' and Mass'r John say, ' No gen'leman eber say dat one word ;' and Mass'r Richard say, ' Sir, you in my house, and you 'sume on dat position ;' and Mass'r John say he ' mighty soon be in some oder house, and den Mass'r Richard not hab sich 'cuse ; ' and, wid dat, he stamp his foot, and walk off like both sides ob de argument 'long to him."

"Then what, Harriet?"

"Mass'r Richard tear roun' to de stables, and he tole Moke to saddle up Prince, and whilst de poor boy doin' his best, he storm roun' at dis thing and dat thing, till Prince work himself up in a fury, too, and I 'spects dey's both tired out by dis time. Prince he jist reared and kicked and foamed at de mouth, and did all de debil's own horse could do to fling Mass'r Richard, and Mass'r Richard, he de whitest white man any body eber seen. Ki! but de whip come down steady, Miss Phyll."

"O, Harriet, how wretched you do make me."

"Dar isn't a bit need to worry, Miss Phyll. Prince done tried himself wid Mass'r Richard 'fore dis, and he allus come in de stable meek as a lamb. When Mass'r Richard's got dat dumb debil in him, he'd ride a ragin' lion, and bring him home like a lamb."

"It's not that, Harriet; it's not that. But if he meet Master John there will be trouble—and O, the sin of it."

"Dat am true as preachin', Miss Phyll."

"If I could only see John Millard."

"I'll mighty soon go for him, ef you say so."

"No; that will not do."

For Phyllis was aware that such a messenger would only make more trouble. Harriet was known to be her maid, and John was known to be her lover. To do any thing which would give cause for ill-natured remarks was to find Richard the excuse which would permit him active interference. "I must avoid the appearance of evil," she said, anxiously. "What must I do?"

"Clar' I don't know, Miss Phyll. 'Pears like you'se on a bery dangerous road. I reckon you'd best pray for de grace to choose de cleanest, safest steppin'-stones."

"Yes; that is best, Harriet."

But Phyllis was not one of those rash beings who rush into the presence of God without thought or solemnity. Slowly bending, body and soul, she communed with her own heart and was still, until it burned within her, and the supplication came. When she rose from her knees, she was resigned in all things to God's will, no matter what self-denial it involved; and she was not unhappy. For, O believe this truth, the saddest thing under the sky is a soul incapable of sadness! Most blessed are those souls who are capable of lodging so great a guest as Sorrow, who know how to regret, and how to desire, and who have learned that with renunciation life begins.

And Phyllis foresaw that renunciation would be the price of peace. At the commencement of the inquiry with her own soul she had refused to entertain the idea. She had tried to find reasons for seeking some other human adviser than Bishop Elliott, because she feared that he would counsel hard things to her. Ere she slept, however, she had determined to go to him very early in the morning.

But while she was drinking her coffee John Millard entered the room. He took her hands, and, looking sorrowfully into her face, said, "Phyllis, my dearest, it was not my fault."

"I believe you, John."

"And you love me, Phyllis?"

"I shall always love you, for I believe you will always try to deserve my love. But we must part at present. I was just going to ask the Bishop to tell you this. I can trust you, John, and you can trust me. He will tell you what you ought to do. And don't think hard of me if I say 'good-bye' now; for though Richard went to the plantation last night, he may be back any hour, and for my sake you must avoid him."

"Phyllis, you are asking a very hard thing. Richard has said words which I can scarcely ignore. Two or three men have inquired if I was going to put up with them?"

"What kind of men?"

"Captain Lefferts and Jim Wade and—"

"Nay, you need say no more. Will you sacrifice my happiness to the opinion of Captain Lefferts and Jim Wade? Are you their slave? Richard is not himself now; if you permit him to force a fight upon you, you will both sorrow for it all your lives."

"I will go and see the Bishop, and do whatever he tells me. If I need a defender from ill words—"

"You may safely leave your good name in his care, John. And who would dare to dispute a word he said? Dear John, I knew I could trust you. Good-bye, my love!"

He drew her to his breast and kissed her, and with a look of fervent, sorrowful love, was leaving the room, when Richard entered by another door. He intercepted the glance, and returned it to John with one of contemptuous defiant anger. It did not help to soothe Richard that John looked unusually handsome. There was a fire and persuasion in his face, a tenderness and grace in his manner, that was very irritating, and Richard could neither control his hands nor his tongue. He began at once to feel for his pistol. "Why is John Millard here?" he asked of Phyllis. "Answer me that."

"He is here to promise me that he will not put the name of Phyllis Fontaine in the mouth of every drunken gambler and scornful man and woman to satisfy his own selfish, false pride."

"He is too big a coward to fight a gentleman, he prefers fighting half-armed savages; but I propose to honor his behavior with more attention than it deserves—unless he runs away."

"John, dear John, do not mind what Richard says now. He will be sorry for it. If you care for me, ever so little, you will not fight about me.

The shame would kill me. I don't deserve it. I will never marry a man who drags my name into a quarrel. Richard, for our mother's sake, be yourself. Brother, you ought to protect me! I appeal to you! For God's sake, dear Richard, give me that pistol!"

"Phyllis," said John, "I will go. I will not fight. Your desire is sufficient."

"Coward! You shall fight me! I will call you coward wherever I meet you."

"No one, who knows us both, will believe you."

It was not the taunt, so much as the look of deep affection which John gave Phyllis, that irritated the angry man beyond further control. In a moment he had struck John, and John had cocked his pistol. In the same moment Phyllis was between them, looking into John's eyes, and just touching the dangerous weapon. John trembled all over and dropped it.

"Go your ways safely, Richard Fontaine. I could kill you as easy as a baby, but for Phyllis's sake you are safe."

"But I will make you fight, sir;" and as he uttered the threat, he attempted to push Phyllis aside. Ere one could have spoken, she had faced Richard and fallen Her movement in some way had fired the cocked pistol, and, with a cry of horror, he flung it from him. John lifted her. Already the blood was staining the snowy muslin that covered her breast. But she was conscious.

"Kiss me, John, and go. It was an accident, an accident, dear. Remember that."

"Stay with her, Richard. I will go for a doctor, my horse is saddled at the door;" and John rode away, as men ride between life and death. Richard sat in a stupor of grief, supporting the white form that tried to smile upon him, until the eyes closed in a death-like unconsciousness.

CHAPTER VI.

"Who redeemeth thy life from destruction."

"Strike—for your altars and your fires;
Strike—for the green graves of your sires;
God, and your native land!"

THE hours that followed were full of suffering to the heart. John came back with the doctors he summoned, and during their investigation he walked restlessly up and down the room in which the tragedy had occurred. Richard never noticed him. He sat in a chair by the open window, with his head in his hands, quite overcome by grief and remorse. It was in John's strong arms Phyllis had been carried to her own room, and no one now disputed his right to watch and to wait for the doctors' verdict. He was very white; white through all the tan of wind and sun; and, as he paced the room, he wrung his hands in an agony beyond speech. Terrible, indeed, to both men was the silent house, with the faint noises of hurried footsteps and closing doors up stairs! What a mockery seemed the cool, clear sunshine outside! What a strange sadness there was in the call of the crickets, and the faint blooms of the last few flowers! There are scenes and sounds which, as backgrounds to great events in life, photograph themselves in their smallest details upon the mind. In the midst of his distress John could not help noticing the pattern of the wall-paper, and the rustling of the dropping leaves and nuts in the garden.

He pitied Richard; for, even in the depth of his own sorrow, he perceived a grief he could not touch —the anguish of a remorse which might have no end in this life. As the doctors came down stairs John went to meet them, for even a minute's reprieve from his torturing anxiety was worth going for. The foremost made a slight movement, a motion of the lips and eyes which somehow conveyed a hope, and when he heard the words, " She may recover," he hastened back to Richard, and said, " There is a hope for her, and for us. God forgive us!"

Richard never answered a word, and John wandered for hours upon the beach, gazing at the gray melancholy sea, and trying to understand how far he had been to blame.. Perhaps it is in the want of pity that the real *infernal* of Satan consists; for whenever he sees us overwhelmed with sorrow, then he casts into our throbbing heart his fiercest weapons. Doubt, anguish, and prostration of hope, worse than death, assailed him. He tried to pray, but felt as if his cries were uttered to an inexorable silence.

As for Richard, he was so mentally stunned that it was not until he had been taken to Phyllis, and she had whispered, " I shall be better soon, Richard," that a saving reaction could be induced. Then the *abandon* of his grief was terrible; then he felt something of that remorse for sin which needs no material fiery adjunct to make a hell for the soul. The Bishop watched him with infinite pity, but for several days offered him no consolation. He thought it well he should sorrow; he wished him to know fully that humiliation which Jesus exalts, that wretchedness which he consoles, that darkness which he lightens.

So, when he heard him one night, muttering as he walked gloomily up and down, "O that I could forget! O that I could forget!" he answered, "Not so, son Richard. Can you escape eternity by forgetting it? And even for this life to forget is a kind of moral forfeiture, a treason against your own soul. Forget nothing, carry every thing about yourself to God — your weakness, your regrets, and your desires."

"How can the infinite God heed my pitiful regrets and desires?"

"Because he loves men individually; he deals with them soul by soul. You, Richard Fontaine, you, your very self, must go to him. You are not only a sinner in the general mass, but a particular sinner under your own name and in your special person. So, then, for you he has a special pardon. He has the special help you need; the very word of grace, that your soul, and yours only, may be able to understand."

"O that God would pity me!"

"You belong to the God of compassions. He resists the proud, but he comes to abide with the broken in spirit."

"If I was only sure Phyllis would recover!"

"And if not?"

"Then I have no hope for this life or the other."

"God will do what seemeth good to him."

"I do not understand—God seems so indifferent to my cries."

"My son, God's indifference does not exist; and if to comprehend the cross of Christ, you must suffer to extremity, I would not spare you, Richard; though I love you. There are four words that you can say, which will shake the gates of heaven; which will make the Father meet you, and the elder Brother welcome you, and the angels sing for joy. Desolate souls, full of anguish, and yet full of hope, have comprehended them: *Have mercy upon me!*"

But the soul is a great mystery. How often is it called, and will not answer. Richard for many weeks could neither believe, nor yet ardently desire. The hour in which he heard that Phyllis was out of danger was the hour of his spiritual deliverance. Then a speechless, overwhelming gratitude took possession of him. He went into his room, and, amid tears and broken prayers of thankfulness, his heart melted. A wondrous revelation came to him, the revelation of a love greater than his sin. He was lost in its rapture, and arose with the sacred, secret sign of the eternal Father in his soul.

Phyllis saw the change as soon as he knelt down by her side, for his whole countenance was altered. She drew near to him, and kissed him. It was after Christmas, and the days bleak and cold; but a great fire of cedar logs burned in the grate, and Phyllis had been lifted to a lounge near it. She was whiter than the pillow on which she lay, white with that pallor of death which the shadowy valley leaves. But O, what a joy it was to see her there once more, to feel that she was coming back, though as one from the grave, to life again!

After half an hour's happy talk he walked to the window and looked out. It faced the garden and the beach. The trees were now bare, and through their interlacing branches he could see the waters of the gulf. As he stood watching them, a figure came in sight. He knew well the tall erect form, the rapid walk, the pause at the gate, the eager look toward the house. He had seen it day after day for weeks, and he knew that, however cold the wind or heavy the rain, it would keep its watch, until Harriet went to the gate with a word of comfort.

Suddenly a thought came into Richard's heart. He left Phyllis, put on his hat, and walked rapidly down to the gate. John was about fifty yards away, and he went to meet him. John saw him coming and walked steadily forward. He expected unkind words, and was therefore amazed when Richard put out his hand, and said, "John, forgive me."

"With all my heart, Richard." The tears were in his eyes, his brown face flushed scarlet with emotion. He held Richard's hand firmly, and said, "I beg your pardon also, Richard."

"Will you come in and see Phyllis?"

"Do you really mean such a kindness?"

"I do, indeed; if Phyllis is able to see you. Let us go and ask."

Harriet was idling about the parlor, dusting the already dusted furniture as they entered. The face was as impassive as a bronze statue. "Go and ask Miss Phyllis, Harriet, if she is able to see Mr. Millard."

In a minute she was by Phyllis's side. "Miss Phill, honey, Miss Phill, dar's a miracle down stairs, nothin' at all less. Mass'r Richard and Mass'r John sittin' together like two lambs, and Mass'r Richard says, 'Can you see Mass'r John a few minutes?'"

The poetic Greek said, "Destiny loves surprises," and our Christian forefathers called all unexpected pleasures and profits, "Godsends." I think such "Godsends" come often to those who ask them. At any rate, Phyllis was asking this very favor, and even while the supplication was on her lips it was granted her. It was Richard, too, who brought John to her side; and he clasped their hands in his, and then went away and left them together. The solemn tenderness of such a meeting needed but few words. John thought life could hardly give him again moments so holy and so sweet. O, how precious are these sudden unfoldings of loving-kindness! These Godsends of infinite love! He had not dared to expect any thing for himself; he had only asked for the life of Phyllis, and it had been given him with that royal compassion that adds, "grace unto favor."

The happy come back to life easily; and when the snow-drops were beginning to peep above the ground, Phyllis, leaning upon John and Richard, stood once more under the blue of heaven, and after that her recovery was rapid and certain. The months of January and February were peculiarly happy ones, full of delightful intercourse and hopeful dreams. Of course they talked of the future; they knew all its uncertainties, and faced, with happy hearts, the struggle they might have together.

At the termination of John's last service he had possessed about two thousand dollars, but this sum had been already much encroached upon, and he was anxious to find a career which would enable him to make a home for Phyllis. There seemed, however, but two possible ways for John: he must have military service, or he must take up land upon the frontier, stock it, and then defend it until he had won it. He had lived so long the free life of the prairie and the woods, that the crowds of cities and their occupations almost frightened him. For theology he had no vocation and no "call." Medicine he had a most decided repugnance to. Law seemed to him but a meddling in other people's business and predicaments. He felt that he would rather face a band of savages than a constant invasion of shoppers; rather stand behind a breastwork than behind a desk and ledger. The planter's life was too indolent, too full of small cares and anxieties; his whole crop might be ruined by an army of worms that he could not fight. But on the frontier, if there was loss or danger, he could defy it or punish it.

He talked to Phyllis of the healthy, happy life of the prairies; of the joy of encamping in forests, and seeing the sun rise between the leaves; of wandering without hinderance; of being satisfied with little. It was these sweet, unplanted places of earth, these grand wastes of green, unpartitioned off into squares of mine and thine, that attracted John and charmed Phyllis: for her heart was with his. She thought of the little home that was to have a look southward and eastward, and which she was to make beautiful; and no grand dame, with the prospect of royal favor and court splendor, was ever half so glad in her future as Phyllis in her dream of a simple and busy Arcadia. It cannot be said that Richard shared her enthusiasm. In his heart he thought Phyllis "too good" for such a life, and to the Bishop he once permitted himself a little lament on the subject.

"But, son Richard," was the answer, "what kind

of men build up new States and lead the van of the onward march? Are they not the heroes of the republic? brave men of large souls and large views, that go naturally to the front because they are too big for the ranks?"

"I suppose so."

"And, depend upon it, the noblest women in the country will love them and go with them. Blessings upon those women who go into the untrampled lands, and serve God and suckle heroes! We forget them too often. The Pilgrim Mothers are as grand as the Pilgrim Fathers, every whit. The men, rifle in hand, take possession of the wilderness; the women make it blossom like the rose. No woman is too fair, or bright, or clever, or good to be a pioneer's wife. If John Millard had been willing to measure out dry goods, or collect debts, I should have had serious doubts about marrying Phyllis to him. If Phyllis had been unwilling to follow John to the frontier, I should have known that she was not worthy of John."

Three days after this conversation John went to New Orleans with the Bishop. The Bishop was upon Church business. John had heard of the colony which had gone with Stephen Austin to Texas, and wished to make further inquiries; for at this time there were three words upon every lip—Santa Anna, Texas, and Houston. At the beginning of John's visit there had been present in his mind an intention of going from New Orleans to Texas at its close.

He was by no means certain that he would stay there, for he mistrusted a Mexican, and was neither disposed to fight under their orders, nor to hold land upon their title. But he had heard of the wonderful beauty of the country, of its enchanting atmosphere, and of the plenty which had given it its happy name; and there had been roused in him a vague curiosity, which he was not averse to gratify, especially as the sail was short and pleasant.

He left the Bishop on Canal Street, and went to the St. Charles Hotel. As he approached it he saw a crowd of men upon the wide steps and the piazza. They were talking in an excited manner, and were evidently under strong emotion. One of them was standing upon a chair, reading aloud a paper. It was the noble appeal of Sam Houston, "in the holy names of Humanity and Liberty," for help. Travis and his brave little band had fallen, like heroes, every soul of them at his post, in the Alamo. Fannin and his five hundred had just been massacred in cold blood, and in defiance of every law of warfare and humanity; and between the Anglo-Americans and a brutal, slaughtering army there was only Houston and a few hundred desperate men. The New Orleans Greys and a company of young Southern gentlemen from Mobile had just sailed. Every man's heart was on fire for this young republic of Texas. Her shield was scarcely one month old, and yet it had been bathed in the blood of a thousand martyrs for freedom, and riddled with the bullets of an alien foe.

John caught fire as spirit catches fire. His blood boiled as he listened, his fingers were handling his weapons. He must see Phyllis and go. That little band of eight hundred Americans gathered round Sam Houston, and defying Santa Anna to enslave them, filled his mind. He could see them retreating across the country, always interposing themselves between their families and the foe; hasting toward the settlements on the Trinity River, carrying their wounded and children as best they could. Every man, women, and child called him; and he cast his lot in with theirs, never caring what woe or weal it might bring him.

The Bishop had promised to call at the hotel for him about four o'clock. John went no farther. He sat there all day talking over the circumstances of Texas. Nor could the Bishop resist the enthusiasm. In fact, the condition of the Texans touched him on its religious side very keenly. For the fight was quite as much a fight for religious as for political freedom. Never in old Spain itself had priestcraft wielded a greater power than the Roman priesthood in Texas. They hated and feared an emigration of Americans, for they knew them to be men opposed to tyranny of all kinds, men who thought for themselves, and who would not be dictated to by monks and priests. It was, without doubt, the clerical element which had urged on the military element to the massacre at the Alamo and at Goliad. The Bishop was with his countrymen, heart and soul. No man's eye flashed with a nobler anger than his. "God defend the brave fellows!" he said, fervently.

"I shall start for Texas to-morrow," said John.

"I don't see how you can help it, John. I wish I could go with you."

"If you hadn't been a preacher, you would have made a grand soldier, father."

"John, every good preacher would make a good soldier. I have been fighting under a grand Captain for forty years. And I do acknowledge that the spirit of my forefathers is in me. They fought with Balfour at Drumclog, and with Cromwell at Dunbar. I would reason with the Lord's enemies, surely, John, I would reason with them; but if they would not listen to reason, and took advantage of mercy and forbearance, I would give them the sword of Gideon and of Cromwell, and the rifles of such men as are with Houston—men born under a free government, and baptized in a free faith."

Richard and Phyllis were standing at the garden gate, watching for their arrival; and before either of them spoke, Phyllis divined that something unusual was occupying their minds. "What is the matter?" she asked; "you two look as if you had been in a fight, and won a victory."

"We will take the words as a good prophecy," answered the Bishop. "John is going to a noble warfare, and, I am sure, to a victorious one. Give us a cup of tea, Phyllis, and we will tell you all about it."

John did not need to say a word. He sat at Phyllis's side, and the Bishop painted the struggling little republic in words that melted and thrilled every heart.

"When do you go, John?" asked Phyllis.

"To-morrow."

And she leaned toward him, and kissed him—a kiss of consecration, of love and approval and sympathy.

Richard's pale face was also flushed and eager, his black eyes glowing like live coals. "I will go with John," he said; "Texas is my neighbor. It is a fight for Protestant freedom, at my own door. I am not going to be denied."

"Your duty is at home, Richard. You can help with your prayers and purse. You could not leave your plantation now without serious loss, and you have many to think for besides yourself."

Of the final success of the Texans no one doubted. Their cry for help had been answered from the New England hills and all down the valley of the Mississippi, and along the shores of the Gulf of Mexico and the coasts of Florida. In fact, the first settlers of Texas had been young men from the oldest northern colonies. Mexico had cast longing looks toward those six vigorous States which had grown into power on the cold, barren hills of New England. She believed that if she could induce some of their popula tion to settle within Mexican limits, she could win from them the secret of their success. So a band of hardy, working youths, trained in the district schools of New England and New York, accepted the pledges of grain and protection she offered them, and, with Stephen F. Austin at their head, went to the beautiful land of Western Texas. They had no thought of empire; they were cultivators of the soil; but they carried with them that intelligent love of freedom and that hatred of priestly tyranny which the Spanish nature has never understood, and has always feared.

Very soon the rapidly-increasing number of American colonists frightened the natives, who soon began to oppress the new-comers. The Roman Catholic priesthood were also bitterly opposed to this new Protestant element; and, by their advice, oppressive taxation of every kind was practiced, especially the extortion of money for titles to land which had been guaranteed to the colonists by the Mexican government. Austin went to Mexico to remonstrate. He was thrown into a filthy dungeon, where for many a month he never saw a ray of light, nor even the hand that fed him.

In the meantime Santa Anna had made himself Dictator of Mexico, and one of his first acts regarding Texas was to demand the surrender of all the private arms of the settlers. The order was resisted as soon as uttered. Obedience to it meant certain death in one form or other. For the Americans were among an alien people, in a country overrun by fourteen different tribes of Indians; some of them, as the Comanches, Apaches, and Lipans, peculiarly fierce and cruel. Besides, many families were dependent upon the game and birds which they shot for daily food. To be without their rifles meant starvation. They refused to surrender them.

At Gonzales the people of Dewitt's Colony had a little four-pounder, which they used to protect themselves from the Indians. Colonel Ugartchea, a Mexican, was sent to take it away from them. Every colonist hastened to its rescue. It was retaken, and the Mexicans pursued to Bexar. Just at this time Austin returned from his Mexican dungeon. No hearing had been granted him. Every man was now well aware that Mexico intended to enslave them, and they rose for their rights and freedom. The land they were on they had bought with their labor or with their gold; and how could they be expected to lay down their rifles, surrounded by an armed hostile race, by a bitter and powerful priesthood, and by tribes of Indians, some of whom were cannibals? They would hardly have been the sons of the men who defied King John, Charles I., and George III., if they had.

Then came an invading army with the order "to lay waste the American colonies, and slaughter all their inhabitants." And the cry from these Texan colonists touched every State in the Union. There were cords of household love binding them to a thousand homes in older colonies; and there was, also, in the cry that passionate protestation against injustice and slavery which noble hearts can never hear unmoved, and which makes all men brothers.

This was how matters stood when John Millard heard and answered the call of Texas. And that night Phyllis learned one of love's hardest lessons; she saw, with a pang of fear and amazement, that in a man's heart love is not the passion which swallows up all the rest. Humanity, liberty, that strange sympathy which one brave man has for another, ruled John absolutely. She mingled with all these feelings, and doubtless he loved her the better for them; but she felt it, at first, a trifle hard to share her empire. Of course, when she thought of the position, she acknowledged the beauty and fitness of it; but, in spite of " beauty and fitness," women suffer a little. Their victory is, that they hide the suffering under smiles and brave words, that they resolutely put away all small and selfish feelings, and believe that they would not be loved so well, if honor and virtue and valor were not loved more.

Still it was a very happy evening. Richard and John were at their best; the Bishop full of a sublime enthusiasm; and they lifted Phyllis with them. And O, it is good to sometimes get above our own high-water mark! to live for an hour with our best ideas! to make little of facts, to take possession of ourselves, and walk as conquerors! Thus, in some blessed intervals we have been poets and philosophers. We have spread liberty, and broken the chains of sin, and seen family life elevated, and the world regenerated. Thank God for such hours! for though they were spent among ideals, they belong to us henceforth, and are golden threads between this life and a higher one.

> "When a flash of truth hath found thee,
>   Where thy foot in darkness trod,
> When thick clouds dispart around thee,
>   And thou standest near to God.
> When a noble soul comes near thee,
>   In whom kindred virtues dwell,
> That from faithless doubts can clear thee,
>   And with strengthening love compel;
> O these are moments, rare fair moments;
>   Sing and shout, and use them well!"
> —Prof. Blackie.

Richard was the first to remember how many little matters of importance were to be attended to. The Bishop sighed, and looked at the three young faces around him. Perhaps the same thought was in every heart, though no one liked to utter it. A kind of chill, the natural reaction of extreme enthusiasm was about to fall upon them. Phyllis rose. "Let us say 'good-night,' now," she said; "it is so easy to put it off until we are too tired to say it bravely."

"Go to the piano, Phyllis. We will say it in song;" and the Bishop lifted a hymn book, opened it, and pointed out the hymn to Richard and John.

"Come, we will have a soldier's hymn, two of as grand verses as Charles Wesley ever wrote:

> "Captain of Israel's host, and Guide
>   Of all who seek the land above,
> Beneath thy shadow we abide,
>   The cloud of thy protecting love:
> Our strength thy grace, our rule thy word,
> Our end the glory of the Lord.
>
> "By thy unerring Spirit led,
>   We shall not in the desert stray;
> We shall not full direction need;
>   Nor miss our providential way;
> As far from danger as from fear,
> While love, almighty love, is near."

The Bishop and Richard went with John to New Orleans in the morning. Phyllis was glad to be alone. She had tried to send her lover away cheerfully; but there is always the afterward. The "afterward" to Phyllis was an extreme sadness that was almost lethargy. Many crushed souls have these fits of somnolent depression; and it does no good either to reproach them, or to point out that physical infirmity is the cause. They know what the sorrowful sleep of the apostles in the garden of Olivet was, and pity them. Phyllis wept slow, heavy tears until she fell into a deep slumber, and she did not awaken until Harriet was spreading the cloth upon a small table for her lunch.

"Dar, Miss Phill! I'se gwine to bring you some fried chicken and some almond puddin', and a cup of de strongest coffee I kin make. Hungry sorrow is mighty bad to bear, honey!"

"Has Master Richard come back?"

"Not he, Miss Phill. He's not a-gwine to come back till de black night drive him, ef there's any thing strange 'gwine on in de city; dat's de way wid all men—aint none of dem worth frettin' 'bout."

"Don't say that, Harriet."

"Aint, Miss Phill; I'se bound to say it. Look at Mass'r John! gwine off all in a moment like; mighty cur'ous perceeding—mighty cur'ous!"

"He has gone to fight in a grand cause."

"Dat's jist what dey all say. Let any one beat a drum a thousand miles off, and dey's all on de rampage to follow it."

"The Bishop thought Master John right to go."

"Bless your heart, Miss Phill! De Bishop! De Bishop! He don't know no more 'an a baby 'bout dis world! You should ha' seen de way he take up and put down Mass'r John's rifle. Mighty onwillin' he was to put it down—kind ob slow like. I wouldn't trust de Bishop wid no rifle ef dar was any fightin' gwine on 'bout whar he was. De Bishop! He's jist de same as all de rest, Miss Phill. Dar, honey! here's de chicken and de coffee; don't you spile your appetite frettin' 'bout any of dem."

"I wish Master Richard was home."

"No wonder; for dar isn't a mite ob certainty 'bout his 'tentions. He jist as like to go off wid a lot ob soldiers as any of de boys, only he's so mighty keerful ob you, Miss Phill; and den he's 'spectin' a letter; for de last words he say to me was, 'Take care ob de mail, Harriet.' De letter come, too. Moke didn't want to gib it up, but I 'sisted upon it. Moke is kind ob plottin' in his temper. He thought Mass'r Richard would gib him a quarter, mebbe a half-dollar."

"Did you think so, also, Harriet?"

"Dem's de house perquisites, Miss Phill. Moke has nothin' 't all to do wid de house perquisites."

"Moke has been sick, has he not?"

"Had de fever, he says."

"Is he not one of your classmates? I think I have heard you say he was 'a powerful member' of Uncle Isaac's class."

"'Clar to gracious, Miss Phill, I forgot dat. Brudder Moke kin hab de letter and de perquisite."

"I was sure you would feel that way, Harriet."

"I'd rather hab you look at me dat shinin' kind ob way dan hab a dollar; dat I would, Miss Phill."

Moke got the perquisite and Richard got his letter, but it did not seem to give him much pleasure. Phyllis noticed that after reading it he was unhappy and troubled. He took an hour's promenade on the piazza, and then sat down beside her. "Phyllis," he said, "we have both been unfortunate in our love. You stooped too low, and I looked too high. John has not money enough; Elizabeth has too much."

"You are wronging both Elizabeth and John. What has Elizabeth done or said?"

"There is a change in her, though I cannot define it. Her letters are less frequent; they are shorter; they are full of Antony and his wild, ambitious schemes. They keep the form, but they lack the spirit, of her first letters."

"It is nearly two years since you parted."

"Yes."

"Go and see her. Absence does not make the heart grow fonder. If it did, we should never forget the dead. Those who touch us move us. Go and see Elizabeth again. Women worth loving want wooing."

"Will you go with me?"

"Do not ask me. I doubt whether I could bear the tossing to and fro for so many days, and I want to stay where I can hear from John."

There was much further talk upon the subject, but the end of it was that Richard sailed for England in the early summer. He hardly expected to renew the enthusiasm of his first visit, and he was prepared for changes; and, perhaps, he felt the changes more because those to whom they had come slowly and separately were hardly conscious of them. Elizabeth was a different woman, although she would have denied it. Her character had matured, and was, perhaps, less winning. She had fully accepted the position of heiress of Hallam, and Richard could feel that it was a controlling influence in her life. Physically she was much handsomer, stately as a queen, fair and radiant, and "most divinely tall."

She drove into Leeds to meet the stage which brought Richard, and was quite as demonstrative as he had any right to expect; but he felt abashed slightly by her air of calm authority. He forgot that when he had seen her first she was in a comparatively dependent position, and that she was now prospective lady of the manor. It was quite natural that she should have taken on a little dignity, and it was not natural that she should all at once discard it for her lover.

The squire, too, was changed, sadly changed; for he had had a fall in the hunting field, and had never recovered from its effects. He limped to the door to meet Richard, and spoke in his old hearty way, but Richard was pained to see him, so pale and broken.

"Thou's welcome beyond ivery thing, Richard," he said, warmly. "If ta hed brought Phyllis, I'd hev given thee a double welcome. I'd hev liked to hev seen her bonny face again afore I go t' way I'll nivver come back."

"She was not strong enough to bear the journey."

"Yonder shooting was a bad bit o' work. I've nowt against a gun, but dash pistols! They're blackguardly weapons for a gentleman to carry about; 'specially where women are around."

"You are quite right, uncle. That pistol-shot cost me many a day's heart-ache."

"And t' poor little lass hed to suffer, too! Well, well, we thought about her above a bit."

Elizabeth had spoken of company, but in the joy and excitement of meeting her again, Richard had asked no questions about it. It proved to be Antony's intended wife, Lady Evelyn Darragh, daughter of an Irish nobleman. Richard, without admiring her, watched her with interest. She was tall and pale, with a transparent aquiline nose and preternaturally large eyes. Her moods were alternations of immoderate mirth and immoderate depression. "She expects too much of life," thought Richard, "and if she is disappointed, she will proudly turn away and silently die." She had no fortune, but Antony was ambitious for something more than mere money. For the carrying out of his financial schemes he wanted influence, rank, and the prestige of a name. The Earl of Darragh had a large family, and little to give them, and Lady Evelyn having been selected by the promising young financier, she was not permitted to decline the hand he offered her.

So it happened she was stopping at Hallam, and she brought a change into the atmosphere of the place. The squire was anxious, fearful of his son's undertakings, and yet partly proud of his commercial and social recognition. But the good-natured evenness of his happy temperament was quite gone.

Elizabeth, too, had little cares and hospitable duties; she was often busy and often pre-occupied. It was necessary to have a great deal of company, and Richard perceived that among the usual visitors at Hallam he had more than one rival. But in this respect he had no fault to find with Elizabeth. She treated all with equal regard and to Richard alone unbent the proud sufficiency of her manner. And yet he was unhappy and dissatisfied. It was not the Elizabeth he had wooed and dreamed about. And he did not find that he reached any more satisfactory results than he had done by letter. Elizabeth could not "see her way clear to leave her father."

"If Antony married?" he asked.

"That would not alter affairs much. Antony could not live at Hallam. His business binds him to the vicinity of London."

There was but one new hope, and that was but a far probability. Antony had requested permission to repay, as soon as he was able, the £50,000, and resume his right as heir of Hallam. When he was able to do this Elizabeth would be freed from the duties which specially pertained to the property. As to her father's claim upon her, that could only end with his or her own life. Not even if Antony's wife was mistress of Hallam would she leave the squire, if he wished or needed her love.

And Elizabeth was rather hurt that Richard could not see the conditions as reasonable a service as she did.

"You may trust me," she said, "for ten, for twenty years; is not that enough?"

"No, it is not enough," he answered, warmly. "I want you now. If you loved me, you would leave all and come with me. That is how Phyllis loves John Millard."

"I think you are mistaken. If you were sick, and needed Phyllis for your comfort, or for your business, she would not leave you. Men may leave father and mother for their wives, that is their duty: but women have a higher commandment given them. It may be an unwritten Scripture, but it is in every good daughter's heart, Richard."

The squire did not again name to him the succession to Hallam. Antony's proposal had become the dearest hope of the old man's heart. He wished to live that he might see the estate honorably restored to his son. He had fully determined that it should go to Elizabeth, unless Antony paid the uttermost farthing of its redemption; but if he did this, then he believed that it might be safely entrusted to him. For a man may be reckless with money or land which he acquires by inheritance, but he usually prizes what he buys with money which he himself earns.

Therefore Richard's and Elizabeth's hopes hung upon Antony's success; and with such consolation as he could gather from this probability, and from Elizabeth's assurance of fidelity to him, he was obliged to content himself.

CHAPTER VII.

"For freedom's battle, once begun,
Bequeathed by bleeding sire to son,
Though baffled oft, is ever won."

"The unconquerable mind, and freedom's holy flame."

"With freedom's soil beneath our feet,
And freedom's banner streaming o'er us."

"And the King hath laid his hand
 On the watcher's head;
Till the heart that was worn and sad,
 Is quiet and comforted."

IT was a beautiful day at the close of May, 1836, and New Orleans was holding a jubilant holiday. The streets were full of flowers and gay with flying flags; bells were ringing and bands of music playing; and at the earliest dawn the levee was black with a dense crowd of excited men. In the shaded balconies beautiful women were watching; and on the streets there was the constant chatter of gaudily turbaned negresses, and the rollicking guffaws of the darkies, who had nothing to do but laugh and be merry.

New Orleans in those days took naturally to a holiday; and a very little excuse made her put on her festal garments, and this day she had the very best of reasons for her rejoicing. The hero of San Jacinto was coming to be her guest, and though he was at death's door with his long-neglected wound, she was determined to meet him with songs of triumph. As he was carried in his cot through the crowded streets to the house of the physician who was to attend to his shattered bone, shouts of acclamation rent the air. Men and women and little children pressed to the cotside, to touch his hand, or to look upon his noble, emaciated face. And though he had striven with things impossible, and was worn to a shadow with pain and fever, he must have felt that "welcome" an over-payment for all his toil and suffering.

Yet it was not alone General Houston that was honored that day by the men of New Orleans. He represented to them the heroes of the Texan Thermopylæ at the Alamo, the brave five hundred who had fallen in cold-blooded massacre at Goliad, and the seven hundred who had stood for liberty and the inalienable rights of manhood at San Jacinto. He was not only Sam Houston; he was the ideal in whom men honored all the noblest sentiments of humanity.

A few friends accompanied him, and among them John Millard. On reaching Texas John had gone at once to Houston's side; and in days and nights of such extremity as they shared together, friendship grows rapidly. Houston, like the best of great generals, had immense personal magnetism, and drew close to him the brave and the honest-hearted. John gave him the love of a son for a father, and the homage of a soldier for a great leader. He rode by his side to victory, and he could not bear to leave him when he was in suffering and danger.

Phyllis expected John, and the Bishop went into the city to meet him. O, how happy she was! She went from room to room re-arranging the lace curtains, and placing every chair and couch in its prettiest position. The table on such holidays is a kind of altar, and she spread it with the snowiest damask, the clearest crystal, and the brightest silver. She made it beautiful with fresh cool ferns and budding roses. Outside Nature had done her part. The orange-trees filled the air with subtle fragrance, and the warm south wind wafted it in waves of perfume through the open doors and windows. Every vine was in its first beauty, every tree and shrub had as yet its spring grace, that luminous emerald transparency which seems to make the very atmosphere green. The garden was wearing all its lilies and pansies and sweet violets, and the birds were building, and shedding song upon every tree-top.

To meet her lover, when that lover comes back from the battle-field with the light of victory on his brow, what women will not put on all her beautiful garments? Phyllis's dark eyes held a wonderfully tender light, and the soft, rich pallor of her complexion took just the shadow of color from the dress of pale pink which fell in flowing lines to her small sandaled feet. A few white narcissus were at her belt and in her black hair, and a fairer picture of pure and graceful womanhood never gladdened a lover's heart.

John had taken in and taken on, even in the few weeks of his absence, some of that peculiar air of independence which seems to be the spirit infusing every thing in Texan land. "I can't help it," he said, with a laugh; "it's in the air; the very winds are full of freedom; they know nothing will challenge them, and they go roving over the prairies with a sound like a song."

The Bishop had come back with John, but the Bishop was one of those old men who, while they gather the wisdom of age, can still keep their young heart. After supper was over he said: "Phyllis, my daughter, let them put me a chair and a table under the live oaks by the cabins. I am going to have a class-meeting there to-night. That will give me the pleasure of making many hearts glad, and it will give John a couple of hours to tell you all the wonderful things he is going to do."

And there, two hours afterward, John and Phyllis went to find him. He was sitting under a great tree, with the servants in little ebony squads around him at the doors of their white cabins; and singularly white they looked, under the swaying festoons of gray moss and in the soft light; for the moon was far up in the zenith, calm and bright and worshipful. John and Phyllis stood together, listening to the close of his discourse, and sharing in the peace of his benediction. Then they walked silently back to the house, wonderfully touched by the pathos of a little "spiritual" that an old negress started, and whose whispering minor tones seemed to pervade all the garden—

"Steal away—steal away!
Steal away to Jesus!"

And in those moments, though not a word was uttered, the hearts of Phyllis and John were knitted together as no sensuous pleasure of dance or song could ever have bound them. Love touched the spiritual element in each soul, and received its earnest of immortality. And lovers, who have had such experiences together, need never fear that chance or change of life can separate them.

"John," said the Bishop, as they sat in the moonlight, "it is my turn now. I want to hear about Texas and about Houston. Where did you meet him?"

"I met him falling back from the Colorado. I crossed the Buffalo Bayou at Vance's Bridge, just above San Jacinto, and rode west. Twenty miles away I met the women and children of the western settlements, and they told me that Houston was a little farther on, interposing himself and his seven hundred men between the Mexican army and them. O, how my heart bled for them! They were foot-sore, hungry, and exhausted. Many of the women were carrying sick children. The whole country behind them had been depopulated, and their only hope was to reach the eastern settlements on the Trinity before Santa Anna's army overtook them. I could do nothing to help them, and I hasted onward to join the defending party. I came up to it on the evening of the 20th of April—a desperate handful of men—chased from their homes by an overpowering foe, and quite aware that not only themselves, but their wives and children, were doomed by Santa Anna to an exterminating massacre."

"What was your first impression of Houston, John?"

"That he was a born leader of men. He had the true imperial look. He was dressed in buckskin and an Indian blanket, and was leaning upon his rifle, talking to some of his men. 'General,' I said, 'I am a volunteer. I bring you a true heart and a steady rifle.'

"'You are welcome, sir,' he answered. 'We are sworn to win our rights, or to die free men. Now, what do you say?'

"'That I am with you with all my soul.' Then I told him that there were two regiments on the way, and that the women of Nashville were raising a company of young men, and that another company would start from Natchez within a week. 'Why, this is great news,' he said; and he looked me steadily in the face till both our eyes shone and our hands met—I know not how—but I loved and trusted him."

"I understand, John. When soldiers are few they

draw close together. Forlorn hopes have their glad hours, and when men press hands beneath the fire of batteries they touch souls also. It is war that gives us our brother-in-arms. The spiritual warfare knows this also, John.

> "'O, these are moments, rare fair moments!
> Sing and shout, and use them well.'"

"The little band were without commissary and without transport; they were half-clad and half-armed, and in the neighborhood of a powerful enemy. They had been living three days upon ears of dried corn, but they had the will of men determined to be free and the hearts of heroes. I told them that the eyes of the whole country were on them, their sympathies with them, and that help was coming. And who do you think was with them, father? The very soul and spirit of their purpose?"

"Some Methodist missionary, doubtless."

"Henry Stephenson. He had been preaching and distributing Bibles from San Antonia to the Sabine River, and neither soldier nor priest could make him afraid. He was reading the Bible, with his rifle in his hand, when I first saw him—a tall, powerful man, with a head like a dome and an eye like an eagle."

"Well, well, John; what would you?

> "'In iron times God sends with mighty power,
> Iron apostles to make smooth his way.'

What did he say to you?"

"Nothing specially to me; but as we were lying around resting and watching he spoke to all. 'Boys!' he said, 'I have been reading the word of the living God. We are his free-born sons, and the name of our elder brother, Christ, can't be mixed up with any kind of tyranny, kingly or priestly; we won't have it. We are the children of the knife-bearing men who trampled kingly and priestly tyranny beneath their feet on the rocks of New England. We are fighting for our rights and our homes, and for the everlasting freedom of our children. Strike like men! The cause commends the blow!'"

"And I wish I had been there to strike, John; or, at least, to strengthen and succor those who did strike."

"We had no drums, or fifes, or banners in our little army; none of the pomp of war; nothing that helps and stimulates; but the preacher was worth them all."

"I can believe that. When we remember how many preachers bore arms in Cromwell's camps, there isn't much miracle in Marston Moor and Worcester fight. You were very fortunate to be in time for San Jacinto."

"I was that. Fortune may do her worst, she cannot rob me of that honor."

"It was a grand battle."

"It was more a slaughter than a battle. You must imagine Santa Anna with two thousand men behind their breastworks, and seven hundred desperate Texans facing them. About noon three men took axes, and, mounting their horses, rode rapidly away. I heard, as they mounted, Houston say to them, 'Do your work, and come back like eagles, or you'll be behind time for the fight.' Then all was quiet for an hour or two. About the middle of the afternoon, when Mexicans are usually sleeping or gambling, we got the order to 'stand ready.' In a few moments the three men who had left us at noon returned. They were covered with foam and mire, and one of them was swinging an ax. As he came close to us he cried out, 'Vance's Bridge is cut down! Now fight for your wives and your lives, and remember the Alamo!'

Instantly Houston gave the order, 'Charge!' And the whole seven hundred launched themselves on Santa Anna's breastworks like an avalanche. Then there was three minutes of smoke and fire and blood. Then a desperate hand-to-hand struggle. Our men had charged the breastwork, with their rifles in their hands and their bowie-knives between their teeth. When rifles and pistols had been discharged they flung them away, rushed on the foe, and cut their path through a wall of living Mexicans with their knives. 'Remember the Alamo!' 'Remember the Goliad!' were the cries passed from mouth to mouth whenever the slaughter slackened. The Mexicans were panic-stricken. Of one column of five hundred

Mexicans only thirty lived to surrender themselves as prisoners of war."

"Was such slaughter needful, John?"

"Yes, it was needful, Phyllis. What do you say, father?"

"I say that we who shall reap where others sowed in blood and toil, must not judge the stern, strong hands that labored for us. God knows the kind of men that are needed for the work that is to be done. Peace is pledged in war, and often has the Gospel path been laid o'er fields of battle. San Jacinto will be no barren deed; 'one death for freedom makes millions free!'"

"Did you lose many men, John?"

"The number of our slain is the miracle. We had seven killed and thirty wounded. It is incredible, I know; and when the report was made to Houston he asked, 'Is it a dream?'"

"But Houston himself was among the wounded, was he not?"

"At the very beginning of the fight a ball crashed through his ankle, and his horse also received two balls in its chest; but neither man nor horse faltered. I saw the noble animal at the close of the engagement staggering with his master over the heaps of slain. Houston, indeed, had great difficulty in arresting the carnage; far over the prairie the flying foe were followed, and at Vance's Bridge—to which the Mexicans fled, unaware of its destruction—there was an awful scene. The bayou was choked with men and horses, and the water red as blood."

"Ah, John; could you not spare the flying? Poor souls!"

"Daughter, keep your pity for the women and children who would have been butchered had these very men been able to do it! Give your sympathy to the men who fell in their defense. Did you see Stephenson in the fight, John?"

John smiled. "I saw him after it. He had torn up every shirt he had into bandages, and was busy all night long among the wounded men. In the early dawn of the next day we buried our dead. As we piled the last green sod above them the sun rose and flooded the graves with light, and Stephenson turned his face to the east, and cried out, like some old Hebrew prophet warrior:

"'Praise ye the Lord for the avenging of Israel, when the people willingly offered themselves.' . . .

"'My heart is toward the governors of Israel, that offered themselves willingly among the people. Bless ye the Lord.' . . .

"'So let all thine enemies perish, O Lord: but let them that love him be as the sun when he goeth forth in his might.'"

"Verses from a famous old battle hymn, John. How that Hebrew book fits itself to all generations! It is to humanity what the sunshine is to the material world, new every day; as cheering to one generation as to another, suitable for all ages and circumstances."

"I asked him where the verses were, and learned them. I want to forget nothing pertaining to that day. Look here!" and John took a little box out of his pocket and, opening it, displayed one grain of Indian corn. "Father, Phyllis, I would not part with that grain of corn for any money."

"It has a story, I see, John."

"I reckon it has. When Santa Anna, disguised as a peasant, and covered with the mud of the swamp in which he had been hiding, was brought before Houston, I was there. Houston, suffering very keenly from his wound, was stretched upon the ground among his officers. The Mexican is no coward. He bowed with all his Spanish graces and complimented Houston on the bravery of his small army, declaring 'that he had never before understood the American character.' 'I see now,' he said, laying both his hands upon his breast, 'that it is impossible to enslave them.' Houston put his hand in his pocket and pulled out part of an ear of corn. 'Sir,' he asked, 'do you ever expect to conquer men fighting for freedom who can march four days with an ear of corn for a ration?' Young Zavala looked at the corn, and his eyes filled. 'Senor,' he said, 'give me, I pray you, one grain of that corn; I will plant and replant it until my fields wave with it.' We answered the request with a shout, and Houston gave it away, grain by grain. Phyllis shall plant and watch mine. In two years one grain will give us enough to sow a decent lot, and, if we live, we shall see many a broad acre tasseled with San Jacinto corn."

"You must take me to see your general, John."

"Bishop, we will go to-morrow. You are sure to like him—though, it is wonderful, but even now he has enemies."

"Not at all wonderful, John. No man can be liked by every one. God himself does not please all; nay, as men are, I think it may stand with divinity to say, He cannot."

"He will like to see you, sir. He told me himself that nearly all the Texan colonies brought not only their religion, but their preachers with them. He said it was these Protestant preachers who had fanned and kept alive the spirit of resistance to Spanish tyranny and to Roman priest craft."

"I have not a doubt of it, John. You cannot have a free faith in an enslaved country. They knew that the way of the Lord must be prepared.

"'Their free-bred souls
Went not with priests to school,
To trim the tippet and the stole,
And pray by printed rule.

"'And they would cast the eager word
From their hearts fiery core,
Smoking and red, as God had stirred
The Hebrew men of yore.'"

During the next two weeks many similar conversations made the hours to all three hearts something far more than time chopped up into minutes. There was scarcely a barren moment, and faith and hope and love grew in them rapidly toward higher skies and wider horizons. Then General Houston was so much relieved that he insisted on going back to his post, and John returned to Texas with him.

But with the pleasant memories of this short, stirring visit, and frequent letters from John and Richard, the summer passed rapidly to Phyllis. Her strength was nearly restored, and she went singing about the house full of joy and of loving-kindness to all living things. The youngest servant on the place caught her spirit, and the flowers and sunshine and warmth all seemed a part of that ampler life and happiness which had come to her.

Richard returned in the fall. He had remained a little later than he intended in order to be present at Antony's marriage. "A very splendid affair, indeed," he said; "but I doubt if Lady Evelyn's heart was in it." It was rather provoking to Phyllis that Richard had taken entirely a masculine view of the ceremony, and had quite neglected to notice all the small details which are so important in a woman's estimate. He could not describe a single dress. "It seemed as if every one wore white, and made a vast display of jewelry. Pshaw! Phyllis, one wedding is just like another."

"Not at all, Richard. Who married them?"

"There was a Bishop, a dean, and a couple of clergymen present. I imagine the knot was very securely tied."

"Was the squire present?"

"No. They were married from the earl's town house. The squire was unable to take the journey. He was very quiet and somber about the affair."

"George Eltham, I suppose, was Antony's chief friend?"

"He was not there at all. The Elthams went to the Continent shortly before the wedding. It troubled the squire."

"Why? What particular difference could it make?"

"He said to me that it was the beginning of a change which he feared. 'George will leave t' firm next. Antony ought to have married Cicely Eltham. I know Eltham—he'll be angry at Cicely having been passed by—and he'll show it, soon or later, I'm sure.'"

"But Antony had a right to please himself."

"I fancy that he had been very attentive to Miss Eltham. I remember noticing something like it myself the summer you and I were first at Hallam."

"Elizabeth says, in her last letter, that they are in Paris."

"Probably they are back in England by this time.

Antony has taken a very fine mansion at Richmond."

"Is the bride pretty?"

"Very—only cold and indifferent, also. I am almost inclined to say that she was sad."

Then they talked of John's visit, and the subject had a great fascination for Richard. Perhaps Phyllis unconsciously described Texas, and Texan affairs, in the light of her own heart; it is certain that Richard never wearied of hearing her talk upon the subject; and the following spring he determined to see the country of which he had heard so much. John met him with a fine horse at the Buffalo Bayou, and they took their course direct west to the Colorado.

To one coming from the old world it was like a new world that had been lying asleep for centuries. It had such a fresh odor of earth and clover and wild flowers. The clear pure air caused a peculiar buoyancy of spirits. The sky was perfectly blue, and the earth freshly green. The sunrises had the pomp of Persian mornings, the nights the soft bright glory of the Texan moon. They rode for days over a prairie studded with islands of fine trees, the grass smooth as a park, and beautiful with blue salvias and columbines, with yellow coronella and small starry pinks, and near the numerous creeks the white feathery tufts of the fragrant meadow-sweet. It looked like miles and miles of green rumpled velvet, full of dainty crinklings, mottled with pale maroon, and cuir, purple, and cream-color.

"How beautiful is this place!" cried Richard, reverently; "surely this is one of the many mansions of our Father! One would be ashamed to be caught sinning or worrying in it!"

As they reached the pine sands the breeze was keener, and their spirits were still more joyous and elastic. The golden dust of the pine flower floated round in soft clouds, and sunk gently down to the ground. Was it not from the flower of the pine the old gods of Olympus extracted the odorous resin with which they perfumed their nectar? And then, shortly afterward, they came to the magnificent rolling prairies of the Colorado, with their bottomless black soil, and their timbered creeks, and their air full of the clean dainty scent of miles of wild honeysuckle.

"Now, Richard, drink—drink of the Colorado. It has a charm to lure you back to Texas, no matter how far away you stray. Soon or later 'the mustang feeling' will seize you, and you'll leave every thing and come back. Do you see yonder hilly roll, with the belt of timber at its foot?"

"Yes, I see it."

"On its summit I am going to build a home—a long, low log-house, spreading out under the live oaks, and draped with honeysuckles. Phyllis helped me to draw the plan of it when I saw her last. The house will be built, and the vines planted by the end of this year. Then she has promised to come. I hope you will be glad, Richard."

"I shall be glad to see her and you happy."

But although the pretty nest was built, and the vines growing luxuriantly, it was not until the close of 1838, nearly two years and a half after San Jacinto, that the lovers could venture to begin their housekeeping. The Indians hung persistently about the timber of the Colorado, and it was necessary to keep armed men constantly on the 'range' to protect the lives of the advance corps of Anglo-American civilization. During this time John was almost constantly in the saddle, and Phyllis knew that it would be folly to add to his responsibility until his service was performed.

As it frequently happens, one change brings another. While the preparations were making for Phyllis's marriage, a letter arrived from Hallam which Richard could not refuse to answer in person. "My father is dying," wrote Elizabeth, "and he wishes much to see you." So the marriage was hurried forward, and took place in the last days of September. Some marriages do not much affect the old home, but that of Phyllis was likely to induce many changes. She would take with her to Texas Harriet and several of the old servants; and there was no one to fill her place as mistress of the house, or as her brother's companion. So that when she thought of the cheery rooms, closed and silent, she was glad that Richard had to leave them, until the first shock of their separation was over.

She went away with a pretty and cheerful eclat. A steamer had been chartered to take the party and all their household belongings from New Orleans to Texas, for Phyllis was carrying much of her old life into her new one. The deck was crowded with boxes of every description; the cabin full of a cheerful party who had gone down to send away the bride with blessings and good wishes. It seemed all sad enough to Richard. After our first youth we have lost that recklessness of change which throws off the old and welcomes the new without regret. The past had been so happy, what the future might be none could tell.

He turned his face eastward without much hope. Elizabeth's letter had been short and inexplicit. "She would see him soon; letters never fully explained any thing." He arrived at Hallam toward the end of October, and having come by an earlier packet than had been named, he was not expected, and there was no one at the coach to meet him. It was one of those dying days of summer when there is a pale haze over the brown bare fields of the gathered harvests. Elizabeth was walking on the terrace; he saw her turn and come unconsciously toward him. She was pale and worn, and an inexpressible sadness was in her face. But the surprise revealed the full beauty and tenderness of her soul. "O, Richard! Richard! my love! my love!" and so saying, she came forward with hands outstretched and level palms; and the rose came blushing into her cheeks, and the love-light into her eyes; and when Richard kissed her, she whispered, "Thank God you are come! I am so glad!"

People are apt to suppose that in old countries and among the wealthy classes years come and go and leave few traces. The fact is that no family is precisely in the same circumstances after an interval of a year or two. Gold cannot bar the door against sorrow, and tapestry and eider-down have no covenant with change. Richard had not been many hours in Hallam when he felt the influence of unusual currents and the want of customary ones. The squire's face no longer made a kind of sunshine in the big, low rooms and on the pleasant terraces. He was confined to his own apartments, and there Richard went to talk to him.

But he was facing death with a calm and grand simplicity. "I'd hev liked to hev lived a bit longer, Richard, if it hed been *His will;* but he knows what's best. I s'all answer willingly when he calls me. He knows t' right hour to make t' change; I'd happen order it too soon or too late. Now sit thee down, and tell me about this last fight for liberty. Phyllis hes fair made my old heart burn and beat to t' vary name o' Texas. I'm none bound by Yorkshire, though I do think it's best bit o' land on t' face o' t' world. And I like to stand up for t' weakest side —that's Yorkshire! If I hed known nowt o' t' quarrel, I'd hev gone wi' t' seven hundred instead of t' two thousand; ay, would I!" Decay had not touched his mind or his heart; his eyes flashed, and he spoke out with all the fervor of his youth: "If I'd nobbut been a young man when a' this happened, I'm varry sure I'd hev pitch'd in and helped 'em. It's natural for Englishmen to hate t' Spaniards and Papists. Why, thou knows, we've hed some tussles wi' them ourselves; and Americans are our children, I reckon."

"Then Texans are your grandchildren; Texas is an American colony."

"They hed t' sense to choose a varry fine country, it seems. If I was young again, I'd travel and see more o' t' world. But when I was thy age folks thought t' sun rose and set i' England; that they did."

He was still able, leaning upon Richard's arm, to walk slowly up and down his room, and sometimes into the long, central gallery, where the likenesses of the older Hallams hung. He often visited them, pausing before individuals: "I seem ta be getting nearer to them, Richard," he said, one day; "I wonder if they know that I'm coming."

"I remember reading of a good man who, when he was dying, said to some presence invisible to mortal eyes, 'Go! and tell my dead, I come!'"

"I would like to send a message to my father and mother, and to my dear wife, and my dead son, Edward. It would be a varry pleasant thing to see a face you know and loved after that dark journey."

"I have read that

> "'Eyes watch us that we cannot see,
> Lips warn us that we may not kiss,
> They wait for us, and starrily
> Lean toward us, from heaven's lattices.'"

"That's a varry comforting thought, Richard. Thou sees, as I draw near to t' other life, I think more about it; and t' things o' this life that used to worry me above a bit, hev kind of slipped away from me."

It seemed to be very true that the things of this life had slipped away from him. Richard expected him every day to speak about Hallam and Elizabeth; but week after week passed, and he did not name the estate. As Christmas drew near he was, however, much excited. Lady Evelyn was expected, and she was to bring with her Antony's son, who had been called after the squire. He longed to see the child, and at once took him to his heart. And he was a very beautiful boy, bright and bold, and never weary of lisping, "Gran'pa."

One night, after the nurse had taken him away, the squire, who was alone with Richard, said, "I commit that little lad to thy care, Richard; see he hes his rights, and do thy duty by him."

"If his father dies I will do all I am permitted to do."

"For sure; I forgot. What am I saying? There's Antony yet. He wants Hallam back. What does ta say?"

"I should be glad to see him in his place."

"I believe thee. Thou wilt stand by Elizabeth?"

"Until death."

"I believe thee. There's a deal o' Hallam in thee, Richard. Do thy duty by t' old place."

"I will. You may trust me, uncle."

"I do. That's a' that is to be said between thee and me. It's a bit o' comfort to hev heard thee speak out so straightfor'ard. God bless thee, nephew Richard!"

He brightened up considerably the week before Christmas, and watched Elizabeth and Lady Evelyn deck his room with box and fir and holly. The young mother was quiet and very undemonstrative, but she attached herself to the dying man, and he regarded her with a pitying tenderness, for which there appeared to be no cause whatever. As she carried away her boy in her arms on Christmas-eve, he looked sadly after her, and, touching Elizabeth's hand, said, "Be varry good to her, wilt tā?"

They had all spent an hour with him in honor of the festival, and about seven o'clock he went to bed. Richard knew that the ladies would be occupied for a short time with some Christmas arrangements for the poor of the village, and he remained with the squire. The sick man fell into a deep sleep, and Richard sat quiet, with his eyes fixed upon the glowing embers. Suddenly the squire spoke out clear and strong—" Yes, father, I am coming!"

In the dim chamber there was not a movement. Richard glanced at the bed. His uncle's eyes were fixed upon him. He went to his side and grasped his hand.

"Did you hear him call me?"

"I heard no one speak but you."

"My father called me, Richard."

Richard fully believed the dying man. He stooped to his face and said, cheerfully, "You will not go alone then, dear uncle; I am glad for your sake!"

"Ay; it's nearly time to go. It's a bit sudden at last; but I'm ready. I wish Antony hed got here; tell them to come, and to bring t' little lad."

There was no disputing the change in the face, the authority of the voice. Gently they gathered around him, and Elizabeth laid the sleeping child on a pillow by his side. Richard saw him glance at the chubby little hand stretched out, and he lifted it to the squire's face. The dying man kissed it, and smilingly looked at Elizabeth. Then he let his eyes wander to Richard and his daughter-in-law.

"Good-bye, all!" he whispered, faintly, and almost with the pleasant words upon his lips he went away.

In a few hours the Christmas waits came singing through the park, and the Christmas bells filled the air with jubilant music; but Squire Henry Hallam had passed far beyond the happy clamor. He had gone home to spend the Christmas feast with the beloved who were waiting for him; with the just made perfect; with the great multitude which no man can number.

CHAPTER VIII.

"We are here to fight the battle of life, not to shirk it."

"The last days of my life until to-day,
What were they, could I see them on the street
Lie as they fell. Would they be ears of wheat
Sown once for food, but trodden into clay?
Or golden coins squandered and still to pay?"

"The only way to look bravely and prosperously forward is never to look back."

ANTONY arrived at Hallam about an hour after the squire's death. He was not a man of quick affections, but he loved his father. He was grieved at his loss, and he was very anxious as to the disposition of the estate. It is true that he had sold his birthright, but yet he half expected that both his father and sister would at the last be opposed to his dispossession. The most practical of men on every other subject, he yet associated with his claim upon Hallam all kinds of romantic generosities. He felt almost sure that, when the will came to be read, he would find Hallam left to him, under conditions which he could either fulfill or set aside. It seemed, after all, a preposterous thing to leave a woman in control of such a property when there were already two male heirs. And Hallam had lately grown steadily upon his desires. He had not found money-making either the pleasant or easy process he had imagined it would be; in fact, he had had more than one great disappointment to contend against.

As the squire had foreseen, his marriage with Lady Evelyn had not turned out well for him in a financial way. Lord Eltham, within a year after it, found a lucrative position in the colonies for his son George, and advised his withdrawal from the firm of "Hallam & Eltham." The loss of so much capital was a great blow to the young house, and he did not find in the Darragh connection any equivalent. No one could deny that Antony's plans were prudent, and dictated by a far-seeing policy; but perhaps he looked too far ahead to rightly estimate the contingencies in the interval. At any rate, after the withdrawal of George Eltham, it had been, in the main with him, a desperate struggle, and undoubtedly, Lord Eltham, by the very negation of his manner, by the raising of an eye-lash, or the movement of a shoulder, had made the struggle frequently harder than it ought to have been.

Yet Antony was making a brave fight for his position; if he could hold on, he might compel success. People in this age have not the time to be persistently hostile. Lord Eltham might get into power; a score of favorable contingencies might arise; the chances for him were at least equal to those against him. Just at this time his succession to the Hallam estate might save him. He was fully determined if it did come into his power never to put an acre of it in danger; but it would represent so much capital in the eyes of the men with whom he had to count sovereigns.

And in his suspense he was half angry with Elizabeth. He thought she must divine his feelings, and might say a word which would relieve them, if she chose. He watched Richard jealously. He was sure that Richard would be averse to his future wife relinquishing any of her rights, and he could scarcely restrain the bitterness of his thoughts when he imagined Richard master of Hallam. And Richard, quite innocent of any such dream, preserved a calmness of manner, which Antony took to be positive proof of his satisfaction with affairs.

At length the funeral was over, and the will of the late squire made known. It was an absolute and bitter disappointment to Antony. "A good-will remembrance" of £1,000 was all that was left him; excepting the clause which enjoined Elizabeth to resell Hallam to him for £50,000, "if it seem reasonable and right so to do." Elizabeth was in full possession, and her father had taken every precaution to secure her rights, leaving her also practically unfettered as to the final disposition of the property.

But her situation was extremely painful, and many openly sympathized with Antony. "To leave such a bit o' property as Hallam to a lass!" was against every popular tradition and feeling. Antony was regarded as a wronged man; and Richard as a plotting interloper, who added to all his other faults the unpardonable one of being a foreigner, "with a name that no Yorkshireman iver did hev?" This public sympathy, which he could see in every face and feel in every hand-shake, somewhat consoled Antony for the indifference his wife manifested on the subject.

"If you sold your right, you sold it," she said, coldly; "it was a strange thing to do, but then you turn every thing into money."

But to Elizabeth and Richard he manifested no ill-will. "Both of them might yet be of service to him;" for Antony was inclined to regard every one as a tool, which, for some purpose or other, he might want in the future.

He went back to London an anxious and disappointed man. There was also in the disappointment an element of humiliation. A large proportion of his London friends were unaware of his true position; and when, naturally enough, he was congratulated on his supposed accession to the Hallam property, he was obliged to decline the honor. There was for a few days a deal of talk in the clubs and exchanges on the subject, and many suppositions which were not all kindly ones. Such gossip in a city lasts but a week; but, unfortunately, the influence is far more abiding. People ceased to talk of the Hallam succession, but they remembered it, if brought into business contact with Antony, and it doubtless affected many a transaction.

In country places a social scandal is more permanent and more personally bitter. Richard could not remain many days ignorant of the dislike with which he was regarded. Even Lord Eltham, in this matter, had taken Antony's part. "Squire Hallam were always varry queer in his ways," he said; "but it beats a', to leave a property like Hallam to a lass. Whativer's to come o' England if t' land is put under women? I'd like to know that!"

"Ay; and a lass that's going to wed hersel' wi' a foreign man. I reckon nowt o' her. Such like goings on don't suit my notions, Eltham."

Just at this point in the conversation Richard passed the gossiping squires. He raised his hat, but none returned the courtesy. A Yorkshireman has, at least, the merit of perfect honesty in his likes and dislikes; and if Richard had cared to ask what offense he had given, he would have been told his fault with the frankest distinctness.

But Richard understood the feeling, and could afford to regard it tolerantly. "With their education and their inherited prejudices I should act the same," he thought, "and how are they to know that I have positively refused the very position they suspect me of plotting to gain?"

But he told Elizabeth of the circumstance, and upon it based the conversation as to their future, which he had been anxiously desirous to have. "You must not send me away again, love, upon a general promise. I think it is my right to understand clearly what you intend about Hallam, and how soon you will become my wife."

She answered with a frank affection that delighted him: "We must give one year to my father's memory; then, Richard, come for me as soon as you desire."

"Say twelve months hence."

"I will be waiting for you."

"You will go with me to New Orleans?"

"I will go with you wherever you go. Your God shall be my God; your home, my home, Richard."

"My dear Elizabeth! I am the proudest and happiest man in the world!"

"And I, Richard; am I not happy, also? I have chosen you freely, I love you with all my heart."

"Have you considered well what you give up?"

"I have put you against it. My gain is incalculably greater than my loss."

"What will you do about Hallam?"

"I shall hold Hallam for Antony; and if he redeem it honorably, no one will rejoice more truly than I shall. If he fail to do this, I will hold it for Antony's son. I most solemnly promised my father to save Hallam for Hallam, if it was possible to do so wisely. He told me always to consult with Whaley and with you; and he has left all to our honor and our love."

"I will work with you, Elizabeth. I promised your father I would."

"I told Antony that I only held the estate for him, or his; but he did not believe me."

"When I come for you, what is to be done with it?"

"Whaley will take charge of it. The income will be in the meantime lawfully ours. Father foresaw so many 'ifs' and contingencies, that he preferred to trust the future welfare of Hallam to us. As events change or arise, we must meet them with all the wisdom that love can call forth."

Perhaps, considering all things, Richard had, after this explanation, as sure a hope for his future as he could expect. He left Hallam full of happy dreams and plans, and as soon as he reached his home began the improvements which were to make it beautiful for his wife. It had its own charm and fitness; its lofty rooms, furnished in cane and Indian matting; its scented dusk, its sweet breezes, its wealth of flowers and foliage. Whatever love could do to make it fair Richard did; and it pleased him to think that his wife would come to it in the spring of the year, that the orange-trees would be in bloom to meet her, and the mocking-birds be pouring out their fiery little hearts in melodious welcomes.

Elizabeth was just as happy in her preparations; there was a kind of mystery and sacredness about them, for a thoughtful woman is still in her joy, and not inclined to laughter or frivolity. But happy is the man whose bride thus dreams of him, for she will bring into his home and life the repose of a sure affection, the cheerfulness of a well-considered purpose. Their correspondence was also peculiarly pleasant. Elizabeth threw aside a little of her reserve. She spoke freely to Richard of all her plans and fears and hopes. She no longer was shy in admitting her affection for him, her happiness in his presence, her loneliness without him. It was easy for Richard to see that she was gladly casting away every feeling that stood between them.

One morning, at the end of October, Elizabeth put on her mantle and bonnet and went to see Martha Craven. She walked slowly, as a person walks who has an uncertain purpose. Her face had a shadow on it; she sighed frequently, and was altogether a different Elizabeth from the one who had gone, two days before, the same road with quick, firm tread and bright, uplifted face. Martha saw her coming, and hasted to open the gate; but when Elizabeth perceived that Ben's wife was within, she said, "Nay, Martha, I don't want to stay. Will you walk back part of the way with me?"

"Ay, for sure! I'll nobbut get my shawl, Miss Hallam. I was turning thee over i' my mind when I saw thee coming. Is there aught wrong?"

"Why do you ask, Martha?"

"Nay, I'm sure I can't tell; only I can see fine that thou ar'n't same as thou was yesterday."

They were just entering the park, and Elizabeth stood musing while Martha closed the gates. Then, after walking a few yards, she said, "Martha, do you believe the dead can speak to the living?"

"Ay, I do. If t' living will hear, t' dead will speak. There's good men—and John Wesley among 'em—who lived w' one foot i' this world, and one in t' other. I would think man or woman hed varry little o' t' next world about 'em, who hed nivver seen or heard any thing from it. Them that hev sat weeping on their bedside at midnight—them that hev prayed death away from t' cradle side—them that hev wrestled a' night long, as Jacob did, they know whether t' next world visits this world or not. Hev you seen aught, Miss Hallam?"

"I have seen my father, Martha. Indeed I have."

"I don't doubt it, not a minute. He'd hev a reason for coming."

"He came to remind me of a duty and to strengthen me for it. Ah, Martha, Martha! If this cup could pass from me! if this cup could pass from me!"

"Honey, dear, what can Martha do for thee? Ivery Christian some time or other comes to Gethsemane. I hev found that out. Let this cup pass, Lord. Didn't I pray that prayer mysen, night and day?"

"Surely, Martha, about Ben—and God let it pass. But he does not always let it pass when we ask him."

"Then he does what is happen better—if we hev t' heart to trust him—he sends an angel to strengthen us to drink it. I hev seen them as drank it wi' thanksgiving."

"O Martha! I am very, very sorrowful about it."

"And varry often, dearie, it is God's will for us to go forward—thou knows what I mean—to make a Calvary of our breaking hearts, and offer there t' sacrifice that is dearest and hardest. Can ta tell me what ta fears, dearie?"

"Just what you say, Martha, that I must pass from Gethsemane to Calvary, and sacrifice there what is my dearest, sweetest hope; and I shall have to bear it alone."

"Nay, thou won't. It isn't fair o' thee to say that; for thou knows better. My word, Miss Hallam, there's love above and below, and strength all round about. If thee and me didn't believe that, O what a thing it would be!"

"Martha, I may need help, the help of man and the help of woman. Can I trust to Ben and you?"

"I can speak for both of us. We'll wear our last breath i' your service. Neither Ben nor I are made o' stuff that 'll shrink in t' wetting. You can count on that, Miss Hallam."

The next evening, just after dusk, Elizabeth was standing at the dining-room window. The butler had just arranged the silver upon the sideboard, and was taking some last orders from his mistress. He was an old man with many infirmities, both of body and temper, but he had served Hallam for fifty years, and was permitted many privileges. One of these was plain speech; and after a moment's consideration upon the directions given him, he said:

"There's summat troubling *them* as are dead and gone, Miss Hallam. If I was thee, I'd hev Mr. Antony come and do his duty by t' land. *They* don't like a woman i' their shoes."

"What are you talking about, Jasper?"

"I know right well what I'm talking about, Miss Hallam. What does t' Bible say? T' old men shall see visions—" He had advanced toward the window to draw the blinds, but Elizabeth, with a face pale as ashes, turned quickly to him and said:

"Leave the blinds alone, Jasper."

She stood between him and the window, and he was amazed at the change in her face. "She's like 'em a'," he muttered, angrily, as he went to his own sitting-room. "You may put a bridle in t' wind's mouth as easy as you'll guide a woman. If I hed been t' young squire, I'd hev brokken t' will a' to bits, that I would. 'Leave t' blinds alone, Jasper!' Highty-tighty, she is. But I've saved a bit o' brass, and I'll none stand it, not I!"

So little do we know of the motives of the soul at our side! Elizabeth was very far, indeed, from either pride or anger. But she had seen in the dim garden, peering out from the shrubbery, a white face that filled her with a sick fear. Then she had but one thought, to get Jasper out of the room, and was quite unconscious of having spoken with unusual anger or authority.

When he had gone she softly turned the key in the door, put out the candles, and went to the window. In a few minutes Antony stood facing her, and by a motion, asked to be admitted.

"I don't want any one to know I have been here," he said, as he stood trembling before the fire. "It is raining, I am wet through, shivering, hungry. Elizabeth, why don't you speak?"

"Why are you here—in this way?"

She could hardly get the words out. Her tongue was heavy, her speech as difficult as if she had been in some terror-haunted dream.

"Because I am going away—far away—forever. I wanted to see you first."

"Antony! My brother! Antony, what have you done!"

"Hush, hush. Get me some food and dry clothes."

"Go to my room. You are safer there."

He slipped up the familiar stair, and Elizabeth soon followed him. "Here is wine and sweet-bread. I cannot get into the pantry or call for food without arousing remark. Antony, what is the matter?"

"I am ruined. Eltham and those Darraghs together have done it."

"Thank God! I feared something worse."

"There is worse. I have forged two notes. Together they make nearly £19,000. The first falls due in three days. I have no hope of redeeming it. I am going to the other end of the world. I am glad to go, for I am sick of every thing here. I'll do well yet. You will help me, Elizabeth?"

She could not answer him.

"For our father's sake, for our mother's sake, you must help me away. It will be transportation for life. O, sister, give me another chance. I will put the wrong all right yet."

By this time she had gathered her faculties together.

"Yes, I'll help you, dear. Lie down and rest. I will go to Martha. I can trust the Cravens. Is it Liverpool you want to reach?"

"No, no; any port but Liverpool."

"Will Whitehaven do?"

"The best of all places."

"I will return as quickly as possible."

"But it is raining heavily, and the park is so gloomy. Let me go with you."

"I must go alone."

He looked at her with sorrow and tenderness and bitter shame. Her face showed white as marble against the dead black of her dress, but there was also in it a strength and purpose to which he fully trusted.

"I must ring for my maid and dismiss her, and you had better go to your own old room, Antony;" and as he softly trod the corridor, lined with the faces of his forefathers, Elizabeth followed him in thought, and shuddered at the mental picture she evoked.

Then she rang her bell, gave some trivial order, and excused her maid for the night. A quarter of an hour afterward she was hastening through the park, scarcely heeding the soaking rain, or the chill, or darkness, in the pre-occupation of her thoughts. She had flung a thick shawl over her head and shoulders, a fashion so universal as to greatly lessen her chance of being observed, and when she came to the park gates she looked up and down for some circumstance to guide her further steps. She found it in the lighted windows of the Methodist chapel. There was evidently a service there, and Martha would be present. If she waited patiently she would pass the gates, and she could call her.

But it was a wretched hour before Martha came, and Elizabeth was wet and shivering and sick with many a terror. Fortunately Martha was alone, and the moment Elizabeth spoke she understood, without surprise or explanations, that there was trouble in which she could help.

"Martha, where is Ben?"

"He stopp'd to t' leaders' meeting. He'll be along in a little bit."

"Can he bring a wool-comber's suit and apron, and be at the gates, here, with his tax-cart in a couple of hours?"

"Yes; I know he can."

"Martha, can you get me some bread and meat, without any one knowing?"

"Ay, I can. Mary 'll be up stairs wi' t' baby, I'se warrant. I'll be back wi' it, i' five minutes;" and she left Elizabeth walking restlessly just inside the gates. The five minutes looked an hour to her, but in reality Martha returned very speedily with a small basket of cold meat and bread.

"My brother, Martha, my brother, will be here in two hours. See that Ben is ready. He must be in Whitehaven as soon as possible to-morrow. Don't forget the clothes."

"I'll forget nothing that's needful. Ben 'll be waiting. God help you, Miss Hallam!"

Elizabeth answered with a low cry, and Martha watched her a moment hastening through the rain and darkness, ere she turned back toward the chapel to wait for Ben.

A new terror seized Elizabeth as she returned. What if Jasper had locked the doors? How would it be possible for her to account for her strange absence from the house at that hour? But Antony had also thought of this, and after the main doors had been closed he had softly undone a side entrance, and watched near it for his sister's return. His punishment begun when he saw her wretched condition; but there was no time then for either apologies or reproaches.

"Eat," she said, putting the basket before him; "and Ben will be at the gates with his tax-cart. He will take you to Whitehaven."

"Can I trust Ben?"

She looked at him sadly. "You must have been much wronged, Antony, to doubt the Cravens."

"I have."

"God pity and pardon you."

He ate in silence, glancing furtively at his sister, who sat white and motionless opposite him. There was no light but the fire-light; and the atmosphere of the room had that singular sensitiveness that is apparent enough when the spiritual body is on the alert. It felt full of "presence;" was tremulous, as if stirred by wings; and seemed to press heavily, and to make sighing a relief.

After Antony had eaten he lay down upon a couch and fell into an uneasy sleep, and so continued, until Elizabeth touched him, and said, softly, "It is time, my dear. Ben will be waiting." Then he stood up and looked at her. She took his hands, she threw her arms around his neck, she sobbed great, heavy, quiet sobs against his breast. She felt that it was a last farewell—that she would never see his face again.

And Antony could not restrain himself. He kissed her with despairing grief. He made passionate promises of atonement. He came back three times to kiss once more the white cold face so dear to him, and each time he kissed a prayer for his safety and pardon off her lips. At the last moment he said, "Your love is great, Elizabeth. My little boy! I have wronged him shamefully."

"He shall be my child. He shall never know shame. I will take the most loving care of his future. You may trust him to me, Antony."

Then he went away. Elizabeth tried to see him from the window, but the night was dark, and he kept among the shrubbery. At such hours the soul apprehends and has presentiments and feelings which it obeys without analyzing them. She paced the long corridor, feeling no chill and no fear, and seeming to see clearly the pictured faces around her. She was praying; and among them she did not feel as if she was praying aloud. She remembered in that hour many things that her father had said to her about Antony. She knew then the meaning of that strange cry on her mother's dying lips—"A far country! Bring my son home!"

For an hour or two it was only Antony's danger and shame, only Antony's crime, she could think of. But when the reaction came she perceived that she must work as well as pray. Two questions first suggested themselves for her solution.

Should she go to Whaley for advice, or act entirely on her own responsibility?

Would she be able to influence Page and Thorley, the bankers who held her brother's forged notes, by a personal visit?

She dismissed all efforts at reasoning, she determined to let herself be guided by those impressions which we call "instinct." She could not reason, but she tried to feel. And she felt most decidedly that she would have no counselor but her own heart. She would doubtless do what any lawyer would call "foolish things;" but that was a case where "foolishness" might be the highest wisdom. She said to herself, "My intellect is often at fault, but where Antony and Hallam are concerned I am sure that I can trust my heart."

As to Page and Thorley, she knew that they had had frequently business transactions with her father. Mr. Thorley had once been at the hall; he would know thoroughly the value of the proposal she intended making them; and, upon the whole, it appeared to be the wisest plan to see them personally. In fact, she did not feel as if she could endure the delay and the uncertainty of a correspondence on the subject.

On the morning of the second day after Antony's flight she was in London. In business an Englishman throws over politeness. He says, "How do you do?" very much as if he was saying, "Leave me alone;" and he is not inclined to answer questions, save, by "yes" or "no." Elizabeth perceived at once that tears or weakness would damage her cause, and that the only way to meet Antony's wrong was to repair it, and to do this in the plainest and simplest manner possible.

"I am Miss Hallam."

"Take a seat, Miss Hallam."

"You hold two notes of my brother's, one purporting to be drawn by Lord Eltham for £9,000; the other by Squire Francis Horton for £9,600."

"Yes; why 'purporting?'"

"They are forgeries."

"My—! Miss Hallam, do you know what you are saying?"

"I do. My brother has left England. He is ruined."

"I told you, Page!" said Thorley, with much irritation; "but you would believe the rascal."

Elizabeth colored painfully, and Mr. Thorley said, "You must excuse me, Miss Hallam—"

"This is not a question for politeness, but business. I will pay the bills. You know I am sole proprietor of Hallam."

"Yes."

"The case is this. If you suffer the notes to be protested, and the law to take its course, you will get nothing. You may punish Mr. Hallam, if you succeed in finding him; but will not the money be better for you?"

"We have duties as citizens, Miss Hallam."

"There has been no wrong done which I cannot put right. No one knows of this wrong but ourselves. I might plead mercy for so young a man, might tell you that even justice sometimes wisely passes by a fault, might remind you of my father and the unsullied honor of an old name; yes, I might say all this, and more, but I only say, will you let me assume the debt, and pay it?"

"How do you propose to do this, Miss Hallam?"

"The income from the estate is about £5,000 a year. I will make it over to you."

"How will you live?"

"That is my affair."

"There may be very unpleasant constructions put upon your conduct—for it will not be understood."

"I am prepared for that."

"Will you call for our answer in three hours?"

"Will you promise me to take no steps against my brother in the interim?"

"Yes; we can do that. But if we refuse your offer, Miss Hallam?"

"I must then ask your forbearance until I see Lord Eltham and Squire Horton. The humiliation will be very great, but they will not refuse me."

She asked permission to wait in an outer office, and Mr. Page, passing through it an hour afterward, was so touched by the pathetic motionless figure in deep mourning, that he went back to his partner, and said, "Thorley, we are going to agree to Miss Hallam's proposal; why keep her in suspense?"

"There is no need. It is not her fault in any way."

But Elizabeth was obliged to remain two days in London before the necessary papers were drawn out and signed, and they were days of constant terror and anguish. She went neither to Antony's house, nor to his place of business; but remained in her hotel, so anxious on this subject, that she could not force her mind to entertain any other. At length all was arranged, and it did comfort her slightly that both Page and Thorley were touched by her grief and unselfishness into a spontaneous expression of their sympathy with her:

"You have done a good thing, Miss Hallam," said Mr. Page, "and Page and Thorley fully understand and appreciate your motives;" and the kind faces and firm hand-clasps of the two men brought such a look into Elizabeth's sorrowful eyes, that they both turned hurriedly away from her. During her journey home she slept heavily most of the way; but when she awoke among the familiar hills and dales, it was as if she had been roused to consciousness by a surgeon's knife. A quick pang of shame and terror and a keen disappointment turned her heart sick; but with it came also a sense of renewed courage and strength, and a determination to face and conquer every trouble before her.

Jasper met her, and he looked suspiciously at her. For his part, he distrusted all women, and he could not understand why his mistress had found it necessary to go to London. But he was touched in his way by her white, weary face, and he busied himself in making the fire burn bright, and in setting out her dinner table with all the womanly delicacies he knew she liked. If Elizabeth could only have fully trusted him, Jasper would have been true as steel to her, a very sure and certain friend; but he resented trouble from which he was shut out, and he was shrewd enough to feel that it was present, though hidden from him.

"Has any one been here while I was absent, Jasper?"

"Ay, Squire Fairleigh and Miss Fairleigh called; and Martha Craven was here this morning. I think Martha is talking wi' Nancy Bates now—she looked a bit i' trouble. It's like Ben's wife hes hed a fuss wi' her!"

"I think not, Jasper. Tell her I wish to see her."

The two women stood looking at each other a moment, Elizabeth trembling with anxiety, Martha listening to the retreating steps of Jasper.

"It is a' as you wished, Miss Hallam."

"Is Ben back?"

"Ay, early this morning."

"Did he meet any one he knew?"

"He met Tim Hardcastle just outside Hallam, *that night*. Tim said, 'Thou's late starting wheriver to, Ben;' and Ben said, 'Nay, I'm early. If a man wants a bit o' good wool he's got to be after it.' This morning he came back wi' tax-cart full o' wool."

"And my brother?"

"He sailed from Whitehaven yesterday."

"To what place?"

"Ben asked no questions. If he doesn't know where Mr. Hallam went to, he can't say as he does. It's best to know nowt, if you are asked."

"O Martha!"

"Hush, dearie! Thou must go and sleep now. Thou's fair worn out. To-morrow 'll do for crying."

But sleep comes not to those who call it. Elizabeth in the darkness saw clearly, in the silence felt, the stir and trouble of a stormy sea surging up to her feet. It was not sleep she needed, so much as that soul-repose which comes from a decided mind. Her attitude toward her own little world and toward Richard was still uncertain. She had not felt able to face either subject as yet.

Two days after her return the papers were full of her brother's failure and flight. Many hard things were said of Antony Hallam; and men forgave more easily the reckless speculation which had robbed them, than the want of manly courage which had made him fly from the consequences of his wrongdoing. It was a bitter ordeal for a woman as proud as Elizabeth to face alone. But she resented most of all that debt of shame which had prevented her devoting the income of Hallam to the satisfaction of her brother's creditors. For them she could do nothing, and some of them were wealthy farmers and traders living in the neighborhood of Hallam, and who had had a blind faith in the integrity and solvency of a house with a Hallam at the head of it.

These men soon began to grumble at their loss, and to be quite sure that "t' old squire would nivver hev let 'em lose a farthing;" and to look so pointedly at Miss Hallam, even on Sundays, that she felt the road to and from church a way of sorrow and humiliation.

Nor could she wholly blame them. She knew that her father's good name had induced these men to trust their money with Antony; and she knew, also, that her father would have been very likely to have done as they were constantly asserting he would—"mortgage his last acre to pay them." And she could not explain that terrible first claim to them, since she had decided to bear every personal disgrace and disappointment, rather than suffer the name of Hallam to be dragged through the criminal courts, and associated with a felon.

Not even to Whaley, not even to Richard, would she tell the shameful secret; therefore she must manage her own affairs, and this would necessarily compel her to postpone, perhaps relinquish altogether, her marriage. Her first sorrowful duty was to write to Richard. He got the letter one lovely morning in November. He was breakfasting on the piazza and looking over some estimates for an addition to the conservatory. He was angry and astonished. What could Elizabeth mean by another and an indefinite delay? He was far from regarding Antony's failure as a never-to-be-wiped-out stain, and he was not much astonished at his flight. He had never regarded

Antony as a man of moral courage, or even of inflexible moral principles, and he failed to see how Antony's affairs should have the power to overthrow his plans.

But Elizabeth positively forbid him to come; positively asserted that her marriage, at a time of such public shame and disapproval, would be a thing impossible to contemplate. She said that she herself had no desire for it, and that every instinct of her nature forbid her to run away from her painful position, and thus incur the charge of cowardice which had been so freely attached to Antony. It was true that the positive sternness of these truths were softened by a despairing tenderness, a depth of sorrow and disappointment, and an avowal of andying love and truth which it was impossible to doubt. But this was small comfort to the young man. His first impulse was one of extreme weariness of the whole affair. He had been put off from year to year, until he felt it a humiliation to accept any further excuses. And this time his humiliation would in a measure be a public one. His preparations for marriage were widely known, for he had spoken freely to his friends of the event. He had spent a large sum of money in adding to and in decorating his home. It was altogether a climax of the most painful nature to him.

Elizabeth had fully released him from every obligation, but at the same time she had declared that her whole life would be consecrated to his memory. Richard felt that the release was just as nominal in his own case. He knew that he never could love any woman but Elizabeth Hallam, and that just as long as she loved him, she held him by ties no words could annul. But he accepted her dictum; and the very fullness of his heart, and the very extremity of his disappointment, deprived him of the power to express his true feelings. His letter to Elizabeth was colder and prouder than he meant it to be; and had that sorrowfully resentful air about it which a child wears who is unjustly punished and yet knows not how to defend himself.

It came to Elizabeth after a day of extreme humiliation—the day on which she called her household servants together and dismissed them. She had been able to give them no reason for her action, but a necessity for economy, and to soften the dismissal by no gift. Adversity flatters no one, and not a soul expressed any grief at the sundering of the tie. She was even conscious, as she had frequently been since Antony's failure, of an air that deeply offended her— a familiarity that was not a friendly one—the covert presumption of the mean-hearted toward their unfortunate superiors. She did not hear the subsequent conversation in the servants' hall, and it was well she did not, for, though the insolence that vaunts itself covertly is hard to bear, it is not so hard as that which visibly hurts the eye and offends the ear.

"Thank goodness!" said Jasper, "I've saved a bit o' brass, and miss may be as highty-tighty as she likes. This is what comes o' lettin' women out o' t' place God put 'em in."

"She's gettin' that near and close," said cook, "I wouldn't stop wi' her for nowt. It's been, 'Ann, be careful here,' and, 'Ann, don't waste there,' till I'se fair sick o' it. She'll not get me to mak' mysen as mean as that. Such like goings on, I nivver!"

"And she's worst to please as iver was!" said Sarah Lister, Miss Hallam's maid. "I'm sure I don't know what's come over her lately. She used to give me many a dress and bit o' lace or ribbon. She gives nowt now. It isn't fair, you know!"

"She's savin' for that foreign chap, that's what it is," said Jasper. "I'll nivver believe but what t' land goes back to t' male heirs some way or t' other. It stands to reason that it should; and she's gettin' a' she can, while she holds t' keys. She'll mak' a mess o' it, see if she doesn't!"

And with this feeling flavoring the household, Elizabeth found the last month of the year a dismal and resentful one. In pursuance of the plans she had laid down for herself, the strictest economy was imperative; for what little she could now save from the plenty of the old housekeeping, might have to see her through many days. At Christmas she bid "good-bye" to every one of her old servants, and even this simple duty had its trial. She stood a hard ten minutes with the few sovereigns in her hand which would be requisite if she gave them their usual Christmas gratuity. Pride urged her to give it; prudence told her, "You will need it." She was not forgetful of the unkind things that would be said of her, but she replaced the money in her desk with this reflection, "I have paid them fully for their service; I must be just before I am generous."

They left early in the day, and for a few hours Elizabeth was the only soul in the old hall. But at night-fall Ben Craven's tax-cart brought his mother, and a few of her personal belongings, and then the village gossips understood "what Miss Hallam was going to do with hersen." Martha took entire charge of the hall, and of all its treasures; and the lonely mistress went to her room that night with the happy consciousness that all she had was in loving and prudent keeping.

It was also a great comfort to feel that she was not under the constant prying of unsympathetic eyes. Elizabeth had suffered keenly from that bitterest of all oppressions, heart-constraint. She often wished to weep, but did not dare. The first servant that entered the room was her master. She owed him a calm expression of face and pleasant words, and if she failed to give them he rent her secret from her. O be certain that every sorrowful soul sighs for the night, as the watchman of Judæa did for the morning. It longs for the shadows that conceal its tears;

it invokes the darkness which gave it back to itself!

With a sense of infinite relief Elizabeth sat in the still house. It was pleasant to hear only Martha's feet going to and fro; to feel that, at last, she was at liberty to speak or to be silent, to smile or to weep, to eat or to let food alone. When Martha brought in her bedroom candle, and said, "Good-night, Miss Hallam; you needn't hev a care about t' house, I'll see to ivery thing," Elizabeth knew all was right, and went with an easy mind to her own room.

Christmas-eve! She had looked forward all the year to it. Richard was to have been at Hallam for Christmas. She had thought of asking Antony and his wife and child, of filling the old rooms with young, bright faces, and of heralding in her new life in the midst of Christmas joys. She had pleased herself with the hope of telling Antony all her plans about "the succession." She had dreamed many a bright dream of her bridal in the old church, and of the lovely home to which she was going soon after the New Year. It was hard to give all up! Still harder to suffer, in addition, misconstruction and visible dislike and contempt.

"Why had it been permitted?" She fell asleep with the question in her heart, and was awakened by the singing of the waits. It was a chill, windy night, with a young moon plunging wildly in and out a sea of black driving clouds. She sat by the fire listening to the dying melody, and thinking of the Christmas-eve when Phyllis stood by her side, and the world seemed so full of happiness and hope. She had had a letter from Phyllis a few days before, a very loving, comforting, trustful letter, and she thought she would read it again. It had been laid within a book which Phyllis had given her, and she brought it to the fireside. It was a volume of poetry, and Elizabeth was not poetical. She could not remember having read a page in this volume, but as she lifted the letter her eyes fell upon these words:

> "The priests must serve
> Each in his course, and we must stand in turn
> Awake with sorrow, in the temple dim
> To bless the Lord by night."

The words affected her strangely; she turned the page backward, and read,

> "It is the night,
> And in the temple of the Lord, not made
> By mortal hands, the lights are burning low
> Before the altar. Clouds of darkness fill
> The vastness of the sacred aisles. . . .
> . . . A few short years ago
> And all the temple courts were thronged with those
> Who worshiped and gave thanks before they went
> To take their rest. Who shall bless
> His name at midnight?
>
> "Lo! a band of pale
> Yet joyful priests do minister around
> The altar, where the lights are burning low
> In the breathless night. Each grave brow wears the crown

Of sorrow, and each heart is kept awake
By its own restless pain: for these are they
To whom the night-watch is appointed. See!
They lift their hands and bless God in the night
Whilst we are sleeping: Those to whom the King
Has measured out a cup of sorrow, sweet
With his dear love; yet very hard to drink,
Are waking in his temple; and the eyes
That cannot sleep for sorrow or for pain
Are lifted up to heaven, and sweet low songs
Broken by patient tears, arise to God.

"The priests must serve
Each in his course, and we must stand in turn
Awake with sorrow in the temple dim,
To bless the Lord by night. We will not fear
When we are called at midnight by some stroke
Of sudden pain, to rise and minister
Before the Lord. We too will bless his name
In the solemn night; and stretch out our hands to him."

And she paused, and lifted a face full of joy and confidence. A new light came into her soul; and, standing up before the Lord, she answered the message in the words of Bunyan, "I am willing with all my heart, Lord!"

CHAPTER IX.

"Walk boldly and wisely in that light thou hast,
There is a hand above will help thee on."

"I deemed thy garments, O my hope, were gray,
So far I viewed thee. Now the space between
Is passed at length; and garmented in green
Even as in days of yore thou stand'st to-day."

"Bless love and hope. Full many a withered year
Whirled past us, eddying to its chill doomsday;
And clasped together where the brown leaves lay,
We long have knelt and wept full many a tear,
Yet lo! one hour at last, the spring's compeer,
Flutes softly to us from some green by-way,
Those years, those tears are dead; but only they
Bless love and hope, true souls, for we are here."

THE strength that had come to Elizabeth with a complete resignation to the will of God was sorely needed and tested during the following week. It had been arranged between herself and Page and Thorley that they should have the whole income of the Hallam estate, deducting only from it the regular cost of collection. Whaley Brothers had hitherto had the collection, and had been accustomed to deposit all proceeds in the banking-house of their brother-in-law, Josiah Broadbent. Elizabeth had determined to be her own collector. The fees for the duty would be of the greatest service to her in her impoverished condition; and she did not wish the Broadbents and Whaleys to know what disposition was made of the revenue of Hallam.

But the Whaleys were much offended at the change. They had so long managed the business of Hallam, that they said the supposition was unavoidable, that Elizabeth suspected them of wronging her, as soon as there was no man to overlook matters. They declared that they had done their duty as faithfully as if she had been able to check them at every turn, and even said they would prefer to do that duty gratis, rather than relinquish a charge with which the Whaleys had been identified for three generations.

But Elizabeth had reasons for her conduct which she could not explain; and the transfer was finally made in a spirit of anger at a supposed wrong. It grieved her very much, for she was unused to disputes, and she could not look at the affair in a merely business light. With some of the older tenants her interviews were scarcely more pleasant. They had been accustomed to meeting one of the Whaleys at "The Rose and Crown Inn," and having a good dinner and a few pints of strong ale over their own accounts. There was no prospect of "makkin' a day o' it" with Miss Hallam; and they had, besides, a dim idea that they rather lowered their dignity in doing business with a woman.

However, Elizabeth succeeded in thoroughly winning Peter Crag, the tenant of the home farm, and a man of considerable influence with men of his own class. He would not listen to any complaints on the subject. "She's a varry sensible lass," he said, striking his fist heavily on the table; "she's done right, to get out o' t' Whaleys' hands. I've been under their thumbs mysen; and I know what it is. I'm bound to do right by Squire Henry's daughter, and I'd like to see them as is thinking o' doing wrong, or o' giving her any trouble—" and as his eyes traveled slowly round the company, every man gravely shook his head in emphatic denial of any such intention. Still, even with Peter Crag to stand behind her, Elizabeth did not find her self-elected office an easy one. She was quite sure that many a complaint was entered, and many a demand made, that would never have been thought of if Whaley had been the judge of their justice.

She had to look at her position in many lights, and chiefly in that of at least five years' poverty. At the New-Year she withdrew her balance from Josiah Broadbent's. It was but little over £600, and this sum was to be her capital upon which, in cases of extra expenditure, she must rely. For she had no idea of letting either the house or grounds fall into decay or disorder. She calculated on many days of extra hire to look after the condition of the timber in the park, the carriages and the saddlery, and the roofs and gutterings of the hall and the outhouses. She had carefully considered all necessary expenditures, and she had tried in imagination to face every annoyance in connection with her peculiar position.

But facing annoyances in reality is a different thing, and Elizabeth's sprang up from causes quite unforeseen, and from people whom she had never remembered. She had a calm, proud, self-reliant nature, but such natures are specially wounded by small stings; and Elizabeth brought home with her from her necessary daily investigations many a sore heart, and many a throbbing, nervous headache. All the spirit of her fathers was in her. She met insult and wrong with all their keen sense of its intolerable nature, and the hand that grasped her riding whip could have used it to as good purpose as her father would have done, only, that it was restrained by considerations which would not have bound him.

In her home she had, however, a shelter of great peace. Her neighbors and acquaintances dropped her without ceremony. The Whaleys had thought it necessary in their own defense to say some unkind things, and to suppose others still more unkind; and it was more convenient for people to assume the Whaleys' position to be the right one, than to continue civilities to a woman who had violated the traditionary customs of her sex, and who was not in a position to return them. But in her home Martha's influence was in every room, and it always brought rest and calm. She knew instinctively when she was needed, and when solitude was needed; when Elizabeth would choose to bear her troubles in silence, and when she wanted the comfort of a sympathizing listener.

Thus the first nine months of her ordeal passed. She heard during them several times from Phyllis, but never one line had come from Richard, or from Antony. Poor Antony! He had dropped as absolutely out of her ken as a stone dropped in mid-ocean. The silence of both Richard and her brother hurt her deeply. She thought she could have trusted Richard if their positions had been reversed. She was sure she would have helped and strengthened him by constant hopeful letters. For a month or two she watched anxiously for a word; then, with a keen pang, gave up the hope entirely. Through Phyllis she learned that he was still in New Orleans, and that he had gone into partnership with a firm who did a large Mexican trade. "He is making money fast," said Phyllis, "but he cares little for it."

It is one good thing in a regular life that habit reconciles us to what was at first very distasteful. As the months went on Elizabeth's business difficulties lessened. The tenants got accustomed to her, and realized that she was neither going to impose upon them, nor yet suffer herself to be imposed upon. The women found her sympathizing and helpful in their peculiar troubles, and there began to be days when she felt some of the pleasures of authority, and of the power to confer favors. So the summer and autumn passed, and she began to look toward the end of her first year's management. So far its record had been favorable; Page and Thorley had had no reason to complain of the three installments sent them.

She was sitting making up her accounts one evening at the end of October. It was quite dark, and very cold, and Martha had just built up a fire, and was setting a little table on the hearth-rug for Miss Hallam's tea. Suddenly the bell of the great gates rang a peal which reverberated through the silent house. There was no time for comment. The peal had been an urgent one, and it was repeated as Martha, followed by Elizabeth, hastened to the gates. A carriage was standing there, and a man beside it, who was evidently in anxiety or fright.

"Come away wi' you! Don't let folks die waiting for you. Here's a lady be varry near it, I do be thinking."

The next moment Martha was helping him to carry into the house a slight, unconscious form. As they did so, Elizabeth heard a shrill cry, and saw a little face peering out of the open door of the carriage. She hastened to it, and a child put out his arms and said, "Is you my Aunt 'Izzy?"

"Then Elizabeth knew who it was. "O my darling!" she cried, and clasped the little fellow to her breast, and carried him into the house with his arms around her neck and his cheeks against hers.

Evelyn lay, a shadow of her former self, upon a sofa; but in a short time she recovered her consciousness and, opening her large, sad eyes, let them rest upon Elizabeth, who still held the boy to her breast.

"I am come to you, Elizabeth. I am come here to die. Do not send me away. It will not be long."

"Long or short, Evelyn, this is your home. You are very, very welcome to it. I am glad to have you near me."

There was no more said at that time, but little by little the poor lady's sorrowful tale was told. After Antony's failure she had returned to her father's house. "But I soon found myself in every one's way," she said, mournfully. "I had not done well for the family—they were disappointed. I was interfering with my younger sisters—I had no money—I was an eye-sore, a disgrace. And little Harry was a trouble. The younger children mocked and teazed him. The day before I left a servant struck him, and my mother defended the servant. Then I thought of you. I thought you loved the child, and would not like him to be ill-used when I can no longer love him."

"I do love him, Evelyn; and no one shall ill-use him while I live."

"Thank God! Now the bitterness of death is passed. There is nothing else to leave."

The boy was a lovely boy, inheriting his father's *physique* with much of his mother's sensitive refined nature. He was a great joy in the silent, old house. He came, too, just at the time when Elizabeth, having conquered the first great pangs of her sorrow, was needing some fresh interest in life. She adopted him with all her heart. He was her lost brother's only child, he was the prospective heir of Hallam. In him were centered all the interests of the struggle she was making. She loved him fondly, with a wise and provident affection.

It scarcely seemed to pain Evelyn that he clung to Elizabeth more than to herself. "He cannot reason yet," she said, "and instinct leads him to you. He feels that you are strong to love and protect him. I am too weak to do any thing but die. She was, indeed, unable to bear his presence long at a time; and his short visits to the silent, darkened chamber were full of awe and mystery to the sensitive child. In a month it became evident that the end was very near. She suffered much, and Elizabeth left her as little as possible. She was quite dependent upon her love, for Elizabeth had notified the dying lady's family of her dangerous condition, and no action of any kind was taken upon the information.

One night Evelyn seemed a little easier, and Harry stayed longer with her. Martha came three times for the child ere she would consent to let him go. Then she took the pretty face in her hands, gave it one long gaze and kiss, and shut her eyes with a painful, pitiful gasp. Elizabeth hastened to her side; but she knew what was passing in the mother's heart, and presumed not to intermeddle in her sorrow. But half an hour afterward, when she saw heavy tears steal slowly from under the closed eyelids, she said, as she wiped them gently away,

"Dear Evelyn, why do you weep?"

"For my poor little wasted life, love; what a mistake it has been. I do not remember a single happiness in it."

"Your childhood, Evelyn?"

"I think it was saddest of all. Children miss happiness most. My childhood was all books and lessons and a gloomy nursery, and servants who scolded us when we were well, and neglected us when we were sick. I remember when I had scarlet fever, they used to put a little water and jelly on a chair beside me at night, but I was too weak to reach them. What long hours of suffering! What terrors I endured from many causes!"

"Forget that now, dear."

"I cannot. It had its influence on all the rest. Then when I grew to childhood I heard but one thing: 'You must marry well.' I was ordered to make myself agreeable, to consider the good of the family, to remember my little sisters, my brothers who had no money and very few brains. It was to be my duty to sacrifice myself for them. Antony saw me; he thought I should be of service to him. My father thought Antony's business would provide for the younger boys. I was told to accept him, and I did. That is all about my life, Elizabeth. I had my dream of love, and of being loved like all other girls, but—"

"But Antony was kind to you?"

"Yes; he was never unkind. He troubled me very little. But I was very lonely. Poor Antony! I can remember and understand now; he also had many sorrows. It was in those days I first began to pray, Elizabeth. I found that God never got tired of hearing me complain; mother scarcely listened—she had so much to interest her—but God always listened."

"Poor Evelyn!"

> "'So I am watching quietly
>   Every day;
> Whenever the sun shines brightly,
>   I rise, and say,
> 'Surely it is the shining of His face!'

I think he will come to-night, Elizabeth."

"You have no fear now?"

"It has gone. Last night I dreamed of passing through a dreary river, and as I stumbled, blind and weak in the water, Christ Jesus stretched out his hand—a gentle, pierced hand, and immediately I was on the shore, and there was a great light whose glory awoke me. When the river is to cross, 'the hand' will be there."

She spoke little afterward. About midnight there was a short struggle, and then a sudden solemn peace. She had touched the hand pierced for her salvation, and the weary was at rest. Elizabeth had promised her that she should be laid in the church-yard at Hallam. There was no opposition made to this disposition of the remains, and the funeral was very quietly performed.

Unfortunately, during all these changes the rector had been away. About a week before Antony's flight he was compelled to go to the south of France. His health had failed in an alarming manner, and his recovery had been slow and uncertain. Many a time, in her various trials, Elizabeth had longed for his support. She had even thought that it might be possible to tell him the full measure of her sorrow. At Evelyn's funeral she missed him very much. She remembered how tender and full of grace all his ministrations had been at her father's death. But the poor little lady's obsequies were as lonely and sad as her life. She was only the wife of an absconding debtor. She had died under the roof of a woman who had seriously offended society by not taking it into her confidence.

It was a cold, rainy day; there was nothing to be gained in any respect by a wretched stand in the wet sodden grave-yard. Even the curate in charge hurried over the service. The ceremony was so pitiably desolate that Elizabeth wept at its remembrance for many a year; and between her and Martha it was always a subject of sorrowful congratulation, that little Harry had been too ill with a sore throat to go to the funeral; and had, therefore, not witnessed it.

The wronged have always a hope that as time passes it will put the wrong right. But it was getting toward the close of the third year, and Elizabeth's trial was no lighter. There had been variations in it. Sometime during the first year an opinion had gained ground, that she was saving in order to pay her brother's debts. As there were many in the neighborhood interested in such a project, this report met with great favor; and while the hope survived Elizabeth was graciously helped in her task of self-denial by a lifted hat, or a civil good-morning. But when two years had passed, and no meeting of the creditors had been called, hope in this direction turned to unreasonable anger.

"She must hev saved nigh unto £10,000. Why, then, doesn't she do t' right thing wi' it?"

"She sticks to t' brass like glue; and it's none hers. I'm fair cap't wi' t' old squire. I did think he were an honest man; but I've given up that notion long sin'. He knew well enough what were coming, and so he left Hallam to t' lass. It's a black shame a' through, thet it is!"—and thus does the shadow of sin stretch backward and forward; and not only wrong the living, but the dead also.

In the summer after Lady Evelyn's death the rector returned. Elizabeth did not hear of his arrival for a few days, and in those days the rector heard many things about Elizabeth. He was pained and astonished; and, doubtless, his manner was influenced by his feelings, although he had no intention of allowing simple gossip to prejudice him against so old a friend as Elizabeth Hallam. But she felt an alien atmosphere, and it checked and chilled her. If she had had any disposition to make a confidant of the rector, after that visit it was gone. "His sickness and the influx of new lives and new elements into his life has changed him," she thought; "I will not tell him any thing."

On the contrary, he expected her confidence. He called upon her several times in this expectation; but each time there was more perceptible an indefinable something which prevented it. In fact, he felt mortified by Elizabeth's reticence. People had confidently expected that Miss Hallam would explain her conduct to him; some had even said, they were ready to resume friendly relations with her if the rector's attitude in the matter appeared to warrant it. It will easily be seen, then, that the return of her old friend, instead of dissipating the prejudice against her, deepened it.

The third year was a very hard and gloomy one. It is true, she had paid more than half of Page and Thorley's claim, and that the estate was fully as prosperous as it had ever been in her father's time. But socially she felt herself to be almost a pariah. The rich and prosperous ignored her existence; and the poor? Well, there was a change there that pained her equally. If she visited their cottages, and was pleasant and generous, they thought little of the grace.

"There must be summat wrong wi' her, or all t' gentlefolks wouldn't treat her like t' dirt under their feet," said one old crone, after pocketing a shilling with a courtsey.

"Ay, and she wouldn't come smilin' and talkin' here, if she'd any body else to speak to. I'm a poor woman, Betty Tibbs, but I'm decent, and I'm none set up wi' Miss' fair words—not I, indeed!" said another; and though people may not actually hear the syllables which mouth such sentiments, it seems really as if a bird of the air, or something still more subtle, did carry the matter, for the slandered person instinctively knows the slanderer.

And no word of regret or of love came from Antony to lighten the burden she was carrying. If she had only known that he was doing well, was endeavoring to redeem the past, it would have been some consolation. Phyllis, also, wrote more seldom. She had now two children and a large number of servants to care for, and her time was filled with many sweet and engrossing interests. Besides, though she fully believed in Elizabeth, she did also feel for her brother. She thought Richard, at any rate, ought to have been treated with full confidence, and half-feared that pride of her family and position was at the bottom of Elizabeth's severance of the engagement. Human nature is full of complexities, and no one probably ever acts from one pure and simple motive, however much they may believe they do.

Martha Craven, however, was always true and gentle, and if any thing more respectful than in Elizabeth's brightest days; and for this blessing she was very grateful. And the boy grew rapidly, and was very handsome and interesting; and no malignity could darken the sweet, handsome room sor the shady, flowery garden. However unpleasant her day among the tenants might have been, she could close her doors, and shut out the world, and feel sure of love and comfort within her own gates.

Things were in this condition in the spring of 1843. But more than £16,000 had been paid, and Elizabeth looked with clear eyes toward the end of her task. Socially, she was as far aloof as ever; perhaps more so, for during the winter she had found her courage often fail her regarding the church services. The walk was long on wet or cold days; the boy was subject to croupy sore throat; and her heart sank at the prospect of the social ordeal through which she must pass. It may be doubted whether people are really ever made better by petty slights and undeserved scorn. Elizabeth had tried the discipline for three years, and every Sabbath evening her face burned with the same anger, and her heart was full of the same resentment. So, it had often come to pass during the winter that she had staid at home upon inclement days, and read the service to her nephew and herself, and talked with the child about the boys of the Old and New Testaments.

And it was noticeable, as indicating the thoughtful loving character of little Harry, that of all the band he envied most the lad who had given his barley loaves to the Saviour. He would listen to Elizabeth's description of the green, desert place, and the weary multitudes, and the calm evening, and then begin to wonder, in his childish words, "How the Saviour looked" at the boy—what he said to him—to fancy the smile of Jesus and the touch of the Divine hand, and following out his thought would say, softly, "How that little boy's heart must have ached when they crucified him! What would he do, aunt? Does the Bible say any more about him?"

But sweet as such Sabbaths were to both woman and child, Elizabeth knew that they deepened the unfavorable opinion about her, and she was sure that they always grieved her old friend. So, one Monday morning after an absence from church, she took the path through the park, determined to call upon him, and explain, as far as she was able, her reasons.

It was a lovely day, and the child walked by her side, or ran hither and thither after a blue-bell, or a primrose; stopping sometimes behind, to watch a pair of building robins, or running on in advance after a rabbit. There was in Elizabeth's heart a certain calm happiness, which she did not analyze, but was content to feel and enjoy. At a turn in the avenue she saw the rector approaching her, and there was something in his appearance, even in the distance, which annoyed and irritated her. "He is coming to reprove me, of course," she thought; and she mentally resolved for once, to defend herself against all assertions.

"Good-morning, Miss Hallam; I was coming to see you."

"And I was going to the rectory. As the park is so pleasant, will you return with me?"

"Yes, I will. Have you any idea why I was coming to see you?"

"I have. It was to say something unjust or cruel, I suppose. No one ever comes to see me for any other purpose."

"Whose fault is that?"

"Not mine. I have done no wrong to any one."

"What has your life been during the last three years?"

"Free from all evil. My worst enemy cannot accuse me."

"Why have you closed the hall? Given up all the kind and hospitable ways of your ancestors? Shut yourself up with one old woman?"

"Because my conscience and my heart approves what I have done, and do. Can I not live as I choose? Am I obliged to give an account of myself, and of my motives, to every man and woman in the parish? O! I have been cruelly, shamefully used!" she said, standing suddenly still and lifting her face, "God alone knows how cruelly and how unjustly!"

"My dear child, people know nothing of your motives."

"Then they are wicked to judge without knowledge."

"Do you not owe society something?"

"It has no right to insist that I wear my heart upon my sleeve."

"I was your father's friend; I have known you from your birth, Elizabeth Hallam—"

"Yet you listened to what every one said against me, and allowed it so far to influence you that I was conscious of it, and though I called on you purposely to seek your help and advice, your manner closed my lips. You have known me from my birth. You knew and loved my father. O, sir, could you not have trusted me? If I had been your friend's son, instead of his daughter, you would have done so! You would have said to all evil speakers, 'Mr. Hallam has doubtless just reasons for the economy he is practicing.' But because I was a woman, I was suspected; and every thing I could not explain was necessarily wicked. O, how your doubt has wounded me! What wrong it has done me! How sorry you would be if you knew the injustice you have done the child of your old friend—the woman you baptized and confirmed, and never knew ill of!"

Standing still with her hand upon his arm she poured out her complaints with passionate earnestness; her face flushed and lifted, her eyes misty with unshed tears, her tall erect form quivering with emotion.

And as the rector looked and listened a swift change came over his face. He laid his hand upon hers. When she ceased, he answered, promptly:

"Miss Hallam, from this moment I believe in you with all my heart. I believe in the wisdom and purity of all you have done. Whatever you may do in the future I shall trust in you. Late as it is, take my sincere, my warm sympathy. If you choose to make me the sharer of your cares and sorrows, you will find me a true friend; if you think it right and best still to preserve silence, I am equally satisfied of your integrity."

Then he put her arm within his, and talked to her so wisely and gently that Elizabeth found herself weeping soft, gracious, healing tears. She brought him once more into the squire's familiar sitting-room. She spread for him every delicacy she knew he liked. She took him all over the house and grounds, and made him see that every thing was kept in its old order. He asked no questions, and she volunteered no information. But he did not expect it at that time. It would not have been like Elizabeth Hallam to spill over either her joys or her sorrows at the first offer of sympathy. Her nature was too self-contained for such effusiveness. But none the less the rector felt that the cloud had vanished. And he wondered that he had ever thought her capable of folly or wrong—that he had ever doubted her.

After this he was every-where her champion. He was seen going to the hall with his old regularity. He took a great liking for the child, and had him frequently at the rectory. Very soon people began to say that "Miss Hallam must hev done about t' right thing, or t' rector wouldn't iver uphold her;" and no one doubted but that all had been fully explained to him.

Yet it was not until the close of the year that the subject was again named between them. The day before Christmas, a cold, snowy day, he was amazed to see Elizabeth coming through the rectory garden, fighting her way, with bent head, against the wind and snow. At first he feared Harry was ill, and he went to open the door himself in his anxiety; but one glance into her bright face dispelled his fear.

"Why, Elizabeth, whatever has brought you through such a storm as this?"

"Something pleasant. I meant to have come yesterday, but did not get what I wanted to bring to you until this morning. My dear, dear, old friend! Rejoice with me! I am a free woman again. I have paid a great debt and a just debt; one that, unpaid, would have stained forever the name we both love and honor. O thank God with me! the Lord, God of my fathers, who has strengthened my heart and my hands for the battle!"

And though she said not another word, he understood, and he touched her brow reverently, and knelt down with her, and the thin, tremulous, aged voice, and the young, joyful one, recited together the glad *benedictus:*

"Blessed be the Lord God of Israel; for he hath visited and redeemed his people,

"And hath raised up a horn of salvation for us in the house of his servant David;

"As he spake by the mouth of his holy prophets, which have been since the world began:

"That we should be saved from our enemies, and from the hand of all that hate us;

"To perform the mercy promised to our fathers, and to remember his holy covenant;

"The oath which he sware to our father Abraham,

"That he would grant unto us, that we, being delivered out of the hand of our enemies, might serve him without fear,

"In holiness and righteousness before him, all the days of our life.

"And thou, child, shalt be called the prophet of the Highest: for thou shalt go before the face of the Lord to prepare his ways;

"To give knowledge of salvation unto his people by the remission of their sins,

"Through the tender mercy of our God; whereby the Dayspring from on high hath visited us,

"To give light to them that sit in darkness and in the shadow of death, to guide our feet into the way of peace."

And Elizabeth rose up with a face radiant and peaceful; she laid upon the table £100, and said, "It is for the poor. It is my thank-offering. I sold the bracelet my brother gave me at his marriage for it. I give it gladly with my whole heart. I have much to do yet, but in the rest of my work I can ask you for advice and sympathy. It will be a great help and comfort. Will you come to the hall after Christmas and speak with me, or shall I come here and see you?"

"I will come to the hall; for I have a book for Harry, and I wish to give it to him myself."

The result of this interview was that the rector called upon the firm of Whaley Brothers, and that the elder Whaley called upon Elizabeth. He attempted some apology at first, but she graciously put it aside: "There has been a mistake, Mr. Whaley. Let it pass. I wish you to communicate with all the creditors of the late firm of Antony Hallam. Every shilling is to be paid and the income of the estate will be devoted to it, with the exception of the home farm, the rental of which I will reserve for my own necessities, and for keeping Hallam in order."

And to Martha Elizabeth said: "We are going to live a little more like the hall now, Martha. You shall have two girls to help you, and Peter Crag shall bring a pony for Harry, and we'll be as happy as never was again! We have had a bit of dark, hard road to go over, but the end of it has come. Thank God!"

"It's varry few as find any road through life an

easy one; t' road to heaven is by Weeping Cross, Miss Hallam."

"I don't know why that should be, Martha. If any have reason to sing, as they go through life, they should be the children of the King."

"It's t' sons o' t' King that hev t' battles to fight and t' prayers to offer, and t' sacrifices to mak' for a' t' rest o' t' world, I think. What made John Wesley, and the men like him, be up early and late, be stoned by mobs, and perish'd wi' cold and hunger? Not as they needed to do it for their own profit, but just because they were the sons o' t' King, they couldn't help it. Christians mustn't complain of any kind o' a road that tak's 'em home."

"But sometimes, Martha, it seems as if the other road was so smooth and pleasant."

"Two roads are a bit different—t' road to Babylon and t' road to Jerusalem aren't t' same. You may go dancin' along t' first; the last is often varry narrow and steep."

"But one can't help wondering why."

"If it wasn't narrow, and varry narrow, too, Miss Hallam, fenced in, and watchmen set all along it, we'd be strayin' far and near, and ivery one o' us going our own way. There isn't a church I knows of—not even t' people called Methodists—as mak's it narrow enough to prevent lost sheep. But it isn't all t' Hill o' Difficulty, Miss Hallam. It isn't fair to say that. There's many an arbor on t' hill-side, and many a House Beautiful, and whiles we may bide a bit wi' t' shepherds on t' Delectable Mountains. And no soul need walk alone on it. That's t' glory and t' comfort! And many a time we're strengthened, and many a time we're carried a bit by unseen hands."

"Well, Martha, those are pleasant thoughts to sleep on, and to-morrow—to-morrow will be another day."

"And a good one, Miss Hallam; anyhow, them as bodes good are t' likeliest to get it. I do think that."

So Elizabeth went to sleep full of pleasant hopes and aims. It had always been her intention to pay every penny that Antony Hallam owed; and she felt a strange sense of delight and freedom in the knowledge that the duty had begun. Fortunately, she had in this sense of performed duty all the reward she asked or expected, for if it had not satisfied her, she would have surely been grieved and disappointed with the way the information was generally received. No one is ever surprised at a bad action, but a good one makes human nature at once look for a bad motive for it.

"She's found out that it wont pay her to hold on to other folks' money. Why-a! nobody notices her, and nivver a sweetheart comes her way."

"I thought we'd bring her to terms, if we nobbut made it hot enough for her. Bless you, Josiah! women folks can't live without their cronying and companying."

"It's nobbut right she should pay ivery penny, and I tell'd her so last time I met her on Hallam Common."

"Did ta? Why, thou hed gumption! Whativer did she say to thee?"

"She reddened up like t' old squire used to, and her eyes snapped like two pistols; and says she, 'Marmaduke Halcroft, you'll get every farthing o' your money when I get ready to pay it.'"

"Thank you, miss," says I, "all the same, I'll be bold to mention that I've waited going on five years for it."

"'And you may wait five years longer, for there are others besides you,' says she, as peacocky as any thing, 'but you'll get it;' and wi' that, she laid her whip across her mare in a way as made me feel it were across my face, and went away so quick I couldn't get another word in. But women will hev t' last word, if they die for 't."

"If she'll pay t' brass, she can hev as many words as she wants; I'm none flayed for any woman's tongue—not I, indeed."

And these sentiments, expressed in forms more or less polite, were the prevailing ones regarding Miss Hallam's tardy acknowledgment of the debt of Hallam to the neighborhood. Many were the discussions in fashionable drawing-rooms as to the propriety of rewarding the justice of Elizabeth's action, by bows, or smiles, or calls. But privately few people were really inclined, as yet, to renew civilities with her. They argued, in their own hearts, that during the many years of retrenchment she could not afford to return hospitalities on a scale of equivalent splendor; and, in fact, poverty is offensive to wealth, and they had already treated Miss Hallam badly, and, therefore, disliked her. It was an irritation to have the disagreeable subject forced upon their attention at all. If she had assumed her brother's debts at the time of his failure, they were quite sure they would have honored her, however poor she had left herself. But humanity has its statutes of limitation even for good deeds; every one decided that Elizabeth had become honorable and honest too late.

And for once the men were as hard as their wives. They had resented the fact of a woman being set among the ranks of great English squires; but having been put there, they expected from her virtues of far more illustrious character than they would have demanded from a man. "For whativer can a woman need wi' so much brass?" asked Squire Horton, indignantly. "She doesn't hunt, and she can't run for t' county, and what better could she hev done than clear an old Yorkshire name o' its dirty trade stain. I'll lay a five-pound note as Squire Henry left her all for t' varry purpose. He nivver thought much o' his son Antony's fine schemes."

"There's them as thinks he left her Hallam to prevent Antony wearing it on his creditors."

"There's them thet thinks evil o' God Almighty himsen, Thomas Baxter. Henry Hallam was a gentleman to t' bone. He'd hev paid ivery shilling afore this if he'd been alive. Yorkshire squires like their own, but they don't want what belongs to other folk; not they. Squire Hallam was one o' t' best of us. He was that."

And though Elizabeth had expected nothing better from her neighbors, their continued coldness hurt her. Who of us is there that has not experienced that painful surprise that the repulsion of others awakens in our hearts? We feel kindly to them, but they draw back their hand from us; an antipathy estranges them, they pass us by. What avail is it to tell them that appearances deceive, that calumny has done us wrong? What good is it to defend ourself, when no one cares to listen? when we are condemned before we have spoken? Nothing is so cruel as prejudice; she is blind and deaf; she shuts her eyes purposely, that she may stab boldly; for she knows, if she were to look honestly at her victim, she could not do it.

But O, it is from these desolate places that heart-cry comes which brings God out of his sanctuary, which calls Jesus to our side to walk there with us. It is in the deserts we have met angels. A great trial is almost a necessity for a true Christian life; for faith needs a soil that has been deeply plowed. The seed cast upon the surface rarely finds the circumstances that are sufficient for its development. And blessed also are those souls to whom the "long watches" of sorrow are given! It is a great soul that is capable of long-continued suffering, and that can bring to it day after day a heart at once submissive and energetic and all vibrating with hope.

Yet it may be fairly said that Elizabeth Hallam was now upon this plane. Her road was still rough, but she was traveling in the daylight, strong and cheerful, and very happy in the added pleasure of her life. Her five years of enforced poverty had taught her simple habits. She felt rich with the £800 yearly rental of the home farm. And it was such a delight to have Harry ride by her side; she was so proud of the fair, bright boy. She loved him so dearly. He had just begun to study two hours every day with the curate, and to the two women at the hall it was a great event every morning to watch him away to the village on his pony, with his books in a leather strap hung at his saddle-bow. They followed him with their eyes until a turn in the road hid the white nag and the little figure in a blue velvet suit upon it from them. For it was Elizabeth's pride to dress the child daintily and richly as the "young squire of Hallam" ought to dress. She cut up gladly her own velvets for that purpose, and Martha considered the clear-starching of his lace collars and ruffles one of her most important duties.

One morning, at the close of January, Elizabeth had

to go to the village, and she told Harry when his lessons were finished to wait at the curate's until she called for him. It was an exquisite day; cold, but clear and sunny, and there was a particular joy in rapid riding on such a morning. They took a circuitous route home, a road which led them through lonely country lanes and across some fields. The robins were singing a little, and the wrens twittering about the hawthorn berries on the bare hedges. Elizabeth and Harry rode rapidly, their horses' feet and their merry laughter making a cheery racket in the lanes. They reached the hall gates in a glow of spirits. Martha was standing there, her round rosy face all smiles. She said little to Elizabeth, but she whispered something to Harry, and took him away with her.

"Martha! Martha!" cried Elizabeth, "you will spoil the boy, and make him sick. What dainty have you ready for him? Cannot I share it? I am hungry enough, I can tell you!"

Martha laughed and shook her head, and Elizabeth, after a word to the groom, went into the parlor. The angels that loved her must have followed her there. They would desire to see her joy. For there, with glowing, tender face, stood Richard. She asked no questions. She spoke no word at all. She went straight to the arms outstretched to clasp her. She felt his tears mingling with her own. She heard her name break softly in two the kisses that said what no words could say. She knew that she had found at last the hour for which she had hoped and prayed so many years.

And Richard could hardly believe in his joy. This splendid Elizabeth of twenty-eight, in all the glory and radiance of her calmed and chastened soul, and her perfected womanhood, was infinitely more charming and lovable than he had ever seen her before. He told her so in glad and happy words, and Elizabeth listened, proud and well-contented with his praise. For an hour he would not suffer her to leave him; yes, it took him an hour, to tell her how well she looked in her riding-dress.

Neither of them spoke of the events which had separated or re-united them. It was enough that they were together. They perfectly trusted each other without explanations. Those could come afterward, but this day was too fair for any memory of sorrow. When Elizabeth came down to dinner she found Harry standing at Richard's knee, explaining to him the lessons he was studying. Her eyes took in with light the picture—the thoughtful gentleness of the dark head, the rosy face of the fair-haired boy.

"I have been showing the gentleman my new book, aunt;" then he bowed to Richard, and, gently removing himself from his arm, went to his aunt's side.

"He says he is called Henry Hallam."

"Yes, he is my brother's only child."

And Richard dropped his eyes; and, turning the subject, said, "I called at the rector's as I came here. He insists upon my staying with him, Elizabeth. He says the hall is not prepared for visitors."

"I think he is right, Richard."

"I brought him a likeness of Phyllis and her husband. I have a similar gift for you."

"No one will prize them more. When did you see Phyllis?"

"A month ago. She is well and happy. John is a member of the Legislature this year. He seems to vibrate between the Senate and the frontier. He is a fine fellow, and they are doing well."

Then they fell into talking of Texas and of the disastrous Santa Fé expedition; and Harry listened with blazing eyes to the tale of cruelty and wrong. Then the rector came and Elizabeth made tea for her guests, and after a happy evening, she watched them walk away together over the familiar road, down the terraces, and across the park. And she went to her room and sat down, silent with joy, yet thinking thoughts that were thanksgivings, and lifting up her heart in speechless gratitude and adoration.

By and by Martha came to her. "I couldn't frame mysen to sleep to-night, Miss Hallam, till I said a word to you. God gave you a glad surprise this morning; that's his way mostly. Hev you noticed that great blessings come when we are nivver expecting 'em?"

"No, I don't think I have; and why should they?"

"I hev my own thoughts about it. Mebbe it isnt allays as easy for God's angels to do *his will* as we think for. T' devil hes angels too, princes and powers o' evil; and I shouldn't wonder if they took a deal o' pleasure in makkin good varry hard to do."

"What makes you think such a strange thing as that?"

"Why-a! I could tell you what looks uncommon like it out o' my own life; but you may tak' your Bible and find it plain as t' alphabet can put it, Miss Hallam. Turn up t' tenth chapter o' t' book o' t' prophet Daniel, and read t' twelfth and thirteenth verses out to me." Then, as Martha stood watching and waiting, with a bright expectant face, Elizabeth lifted the book, and read,

"'Fear not, Daniel: for from the first day that thou didst set thine heart to understand, and to chasten thyself before thy God, thy words were heard, and I am come for thy words. But the prince of the kingdom of Persia withstood me one and twenty days: but, lo, Michael, one of the chief princes, came to help me.'"

"Yet he was an angel, Miss Hallam, whose face was like lightning, and his eyes like lamps o' fire, and his arms and feet like polished brass, and his voice like the voice of a multitude."

"Then you think, Martha, that the Bible teaches

us that evil as well as good angels interfere in human life?"

"Ay, I'm sure it does, Miss Hallam. If God is said to open t' eyes o' our understanding, t' devil is said to blind 'em. Are Christians filled wi' t' Spirit o' God? 'Why,' said Peter to Ananias, 'Why hath Satan filled thy heart?' Does God work in us to will and to do? T' devil also works in t' children o' disobedience. What do you mak' o' that now?"

"I think it is a very solemn consideration. I have often thought of good angels around me; but we may well 'work out our salvation with fear and trembling,' if evil ones are waiting to hinder us at every turn."

"And you see, then, how even good angels may hev to be varry prudent about t' blessings they hev on t' road to us. So they come as surprises. I don't think it's iver well, even wi' oursel's, to blow a trumpet before any thing we're going to do. After we hev got t' good thing, after we hev done t' great thing, it'll be a varry good time to talk about it. Many a night I've thought o' t' words on my little Wesley tea-pot, and just said 'em softly, down in my heart, 'In God we trust.' But to-night I hev put a bit o' holly all around it, and I hev filled it full o' t' freshest greens and flowers I could get, and I s'all stand boldly up before it, and say out loud—'In God we trust!'"

CHAPTER X.

"When we have hoped and sought and striven and lost our aim,
then the truth fronts us, beaming out of the darkness."

"Speaking of things remembered, and so sit
Speechless while things forgotten call to us."

"We who say as we go,
'Strange to think by the way,
Whatever there is to know,
That we shall know one day.'"

"I WOULD tell her every thing."

It was the rector who spoke. He and Richard were sitting before the study fire; they had been talking long and seriously, and the rector's eyes were dim and troubled. "Yes, I would tell her every thing." Then he put his pipe down, and began to walk about the floor, murmuring at intervals, "Poor fellow! poor fellow! God is merciful."

In accord with this advice Richard went to see Elizabeth. It was a painful story he had to tell, and he was half inclined to hide all but the unavoidable in his own heart; but he could not doubt the wisdom which counseled him "to tell all, and tell it as soon as possible." The opportunity occurred immediately. He found Elizabeth mending, with skillful fingers, some fine old lace, which she was going to make into ruffles for Harry's neck and wrists. It was a stormy morning, and the boy had not been permitted to go to the village, but he sat beside her, reading aloud that delight of boyhood, "Robinson Crusoe." Elizabeth had never removed her mourning, but her fair hair and white linen collar and cuffs made an exquisite contrast to the soft somber folds of her dress; while Harry was just a bit of brilliant color, from the tawny gold of his long curls to the rich lights of his crimson velvet suit, with its white lace and snowy hose, and low shoes tied with crimson ribbons.

He was a trifle jealous of Richard's interference between himself and his aunt, but far too gentlemanly a little fellow to show it; and quite shrewd enough to understand, that if he went to Martha for an hour or two, he would not be much missed. They both followed him with admiring eyes as he left the room; and when he stood a moment in the open door and touched his brow with his hand, as a parting courtesy, neither could help an expression of satisfaction.

"What a handsome lad!" said Richard.

"He is. If he live to take his father's or my place here, he will be a noble squire of Hallam."

"Then he is to be your successor?"

"Failing Antony."

"Then, Elizabeth dear, he is squire of Hallam already, for Antony is dead."

"Dead! Without a word! Without sign of any kind—O, Richard, is it really—death?"

Richard bowed his head, and Elizabeth sat gazing out of the window with vacant introspective vision, trying to call up from the past the dear form that would come no more. She put down her sewing, and Richard drew closer to her side, and comforted her with assurances that he believed, "all was well with the dead." "I was with him during the last weeks of his sad life," he said; "I did all that love could suggest to soothe his sufferings. He sleeps well; believe me."

"I never heard from him after our sorrowful farewell. I looked and hoped for a little until my heart failed me; and I thought he perished at sea."

"No: God's mercy spared him until he had proved the vanity of all earthly ambition, and then he gave him rest. When he awoke, I have no doubt that 'he was satisfied.'"

"Where did he die? Tell me all, Richard, for there may be words and events that seem trivial to you that will be full of meaning to me."

"Last March I went to Mexico on business of importance, and passing one morning through the Grand Plaza, I thought a figure slowly sauntering before me was a familiar one. It went into a small office for the exchange of foreign money, and, as I wanted some exchange, I followed. To my surprise the man seemed to be the proprietor; he went behind the counter into a room, but on my touching a bell reappeared. It was Antony. The moment our eyes met, we recognized each other, and after a slight hesitation, I am sure that he was thankful and delighted to see me. I was shocked at his appearance. He looked fifty years of age, and had lost all his color, and was extremely emaciated. We were soon interrupted, and he promised to come to my hotel and dine with me at six o'clock.

"I noticed at dinner that he ate very little, and that he had a distressing and nearly constant cough, and afterward, as we sat on the piazza, I said, 'Let us go inside, Antony; there is a cold wind, and you have a very bad cough.'

"'O, it is nothing,' he answered fretfully. 'The only wonder is that I am alive, after all I have been made to suffer. Stronger men than I ever was fell and died at my side. You are too polite, Richard, to ask me where I have been; but if you wish to hear, I should like to tell you.'

"I answered, 'You are my friend and my brother, Antony; and whatever touches you for good or for evil touches me also. I should like to hear all you wish to tell me.'

"'It is all evil, Richard. You would hear from Elizabeth that I was obliged to leave England?'

"'Yes, she told me.'

"'How long have you been married?' he asked me, sharply; and when I said, 'We are not married; Elizabeth wrote and said she had a duty to perform which might bind her for many years to it, and it alone,' your brother seemed to be greatly troubled; and asked, angrily, 'And you took her at her word, and left her in her sorrow alone? Richard, I did not think you would have been so cruel!' And, my darling, it was the first time I had thought of our separation in that light. I attempted no excuses to Antony, and, after a moment's reflection, he went on:

"'I left Whitehaven in a ship bound for Havana, and I remained in that city until the spring of 1841. But I never liked the place, and I removed to New Orleans at that time. I had some idea of seeing you, and opening my whole heart to you; but I lingered day after day unable to make up my mind.' At the hotel were I stayed there were a number of Texans coming and going, and I was delighted with their bold, frank ways, and with the air of conquest and freedom and adventure that clung to them. One day I passed you upon Canal Street. You looked so miserable, and were speaking to the man with whom you were in conversation so sternly, that I could not make up my mind to address you. I walked a block and returned. You were just saying, " If I did right, I would send you to the Penitentiary, sir; " and I had a sudden fear of you, and, returning to the hotel, I packed my valise and took the next steamer for Galveston.'

" I answered, 'I remember the morning, Antony; the man had stolen from me a large sum of money. I was angry with him, and I had a right to be angry.'

"Antony frowned, and for some minutes did not resume his story. He looked so faint, also, that I pushed a little wine and water toward him, and he wet his lips, and went on:

"'Yes, you had a perfect right; but your manner checked me. I did not know either how matters stood between you and my sister; so, instead of speaking to you, I went to Texas. I found Houston —I mean the little town of that name—in a state of the greatest excitement. The tradesmen were working night and day, shoeing horses, or mending rifles and pistols; and the saddlers' shops were besieged for leathern pouches and saddlery of all kinds. The streets were like a fair. Of course, I caught the enthusiasm. It was the Santa Fè expedition, and I threw myself into it heart and soul. I was going as a trader, and I hastened forward, with others similarly disposed, to Austin, loaded two wagons with merchandise of every description, and left with the expedition in June.

"'You know what a disastrous failure it was. We fell into the hands of the Mexicans by the blackest villainy; through the treachery of a companion in whom we all put perfect trust, and who had pledged us his Masonic faith that if we gave up our arms we should be allowed eight days to trade, and then have them returned, with permission to go back to Austin in peace. But once disarmed, our wagons and goods were seized, we were stripped of every thing, tied six

18

or eight in a lariat, and sent, with a strong military escort to Mexico.

"'Try to imagine, Richard, what we felt in prospect of this walk of two thousand miles, through deserts, and over mountains, driven, like cattle, with a pint of meal each night for food, and a single blanket to cover us in the bitterest cold. Strong men fell down dead at my side, or, being too exhausted to move, were shot and left to the wolves and carrion; our guard merely cutting off the poor fellows' ears, as evidence that they had not escaped. The horrors of that march were unspeakable.'

"You said I was to tell you all—shall I go on, Elizabeth?"

She lifted her eyes, and whispered, "Go on; I must hear all, or how can I feel all? O Antony! Antony!"

"I shall never forget his face, Elizabeth. Anger, pity, suffering, chased each other over it, till his eyes filled and his lips quivered. I did not speak. Every word I could think of seemed so poor and commonplace; but I bent forward and took his hands, and he saw in my face what I could not say, and for a minute or two he lost control of himself, and wept like a child.

"'Not for myself, Richard;' he said, 'no, I was thinking of that awful march across the "Dead Man's Journey," a savage, thorny desert of ninety miles, destitute of water. We were driven through it without food and without sleep. My companion was a young man of twenty, the son of a wealthy Alabamian planter. I met him in Austin, so bright and bold, so full of eager, loving life, so daring, and so hopeful; but his strength had been failing for two days ere he came to the desert. His feet were in a pitiable condition. He was sleeping as he walked. Then he became delirious, and talked constantly of his father and mother and sisters. He had been too ill to fill his canteen before starting; his thirst soon became intolerable; I gave him all my water, I begged from others a few spoonfuls of their store, I held him up as long as I was able; but at last, at last, he dropped. Richard! Richard! They shot him before my eyes, shot him with the cry of 'Christ' upon his lips. I think my anger supported me, I don't know else how I bore it; but I was mad with horror and rage at the brutal cowards.

"'When I reached the end of my journey I was imprisoned with some of my comrades, first in a lazaretto, among lepers, in every stage of their loathsome disease; and afterward removed to Santiago, where, hampered with heavy chains, we were set to work upon the public roads.'

"I asked him why he did not apply to the British consul, and he said, 'I had a reason for not doing so, Richard. I may tell you the reason sometime, but not to-night. I knew that there was diplomatic correspondence going on about our relief, and that, soon or later, those who survived their brutal treatment would be set free. I was one that lived to have my chains knocked off; but I was many weeks sick afterward, and, indeed, I have not recovered yet.'

"So you began the exchange business here?"

"'Yes; I had saved through all my troubles a little store of gold in a belt around my waist. It was not much, but I have more than doubled it; and as soon as I can, I intend leaving Mexico, and beginning life again among civilized human beings.'"

Elizabeth was weeping bitterly, but she said, "I am glad you have told me this, Richard. Ah, my brave brother! You showed in your extremity the race from which you sprung! Sydney's deed was no greater than yours! That 'Dead Man's Journey,' Richard, redeems all to me. I am proud of Antony at last. I freely forgive him every hour of sorrow he has caused me. His picture shall be hung next his father's, and I will have all else forgotten but this one deed. He gave his last drink of water to the boy perishing at his side; he begged for him when his own store failed, he supported him when he could scarcely walk himself, and had tears and righteous anger for the wrongs of others; but for his own sufferings no word of complaint! After this, Richard, I do not fear what else you have to tell me. Did he die in Mexico?"

"No; he was very unhappy in the country, and he longed to leave it. As the weather grew warmer his weakness and suffering increased; but it was a hard thing for him to admit that he was seriously ill. At last he was unable to attend to his business, and I persuaded him to close his office. I shall never forget his face as he turned the key in it; I think he felt then that life for him was over. I had remained in Mexico for some weeks entirely on his account, and I now suggested, as he had no business cares, a journey home by way of Texas. I really believed that the rare, fine air of the prairies would do him good; and I was sure if we could reach Phyllis, he would at least die among friends.

"When I made the proposal he was eager as a child for it. He did not want to delay an hour. He remembered the ethereal, vivifying airs of Western Texas, and was quite sure if he could only breathe them again he would be well in a short time. He was carried in a litter to Vera Cruz, and then taken by sea to Brownsville. And really the journey seemed to greatly revive him, and I could not help joining in his belief that Phyllis and Western Texas would save him.

"But when we reached the Basque there was a sudden change, a change there was no mistaking. He was unable to proceed, and I laid his mattress under a great live oak whose branches overshadowed space enough for our camp. I cannot tell you, Elizabeth, what a singular stillness and awe settled over all of us. I have often thought and wondered about it since. There was no quarreling, no singing, nor laughing among the men, who were usually ready enough for any of them; and this 'still' feeling, I suppose, was intensified by the weather, and the peculiar atmosphere. For we had come by such slow stages, that it was Indian summer, and if you can imagine an English October day, spiritualized, and wearing a veil of exquisite purply-grey and amber haze, you may have some idea of the lovely melancholy of these dying days of the year on the prairie.

"We waited several days in this place, and he grew very weak, suffering much, but always suffering patiently and with a brave cheerfulness that was inexpressibly sorrowful. It was on a Sunday morning that he touched me just between the dawn and the daylight, and said, 'Richard, I have been dreaming of Hallam and of my mother. She is waiting for me. I will sleep no more in this world. It is a beautiful world!' During the day I never left him, and we talked a great deal about the future, whose mystery he was so soon to enter. Soon after sunset he whispered to me the wrong he had done, and which he was quite sure you were retrieving. He acknowledged that he ought to have told me before, but pleaded his weakness and his dread of losing the only friend he had. It is needless to say I forgave him, forgave him for you and for myself; and did it so heartily, that before I was conscious of the act I had stooped and kissed him.

"About midnight he said to me, 'Pray, Richard;'

and surely I was helped to do so, for crowding into my memory came every blessed promise, every comforting hope, that could make the hour of death the hour of victory. And while I was saying, 'Behold the Lamb of God, who taketh away the sin of the world,' he passed away. We were quite alone. The men were sleeping around, unconscious of 'Him that waited.' The moon flooded the prairie with a soft, hazy light, and all was so still that I could hear the cattle in the distance cropping the grass. I awoke no one. The last offices I could do for him I quietly performed, and then sat down to watch until daylight. All was very happy and solemn. It was as if the Angel of Peace had passed by. And as if to check any doubt or fear I might be tempted to indulge, suddenly, and swift and penetrating as light, these lines came to my recollection:

"'Down in the valley of Death,
 A Cross is standing plain;
Where strange and awful the shadows sleep,
 And the ground has a deep, red stain.

"'This Cross uplifted there
 Forbids, with voice divine,
Our anguished hearts to break for the dead
 Who have died and made no sign.

"'As they turned away from us,
 Dear eyes that were heavy and dim,
May have met His look who was lifted there,
 May be sleeping safe in Him.'"

"Where did you bury him, Richard?"

"Under the tree. Not in all the world could we

have found for him so lovely and so still a grave. Just at sunrise we laid him there, 'in sure and certain hope' of the resurrection. One of the Mexicans cut a cross and placed it at his head, and, rude and ignorant as they all were, I believe every one said a prayer for his repose. Then I took the little gold he had, divided it among them, paid them their wages, and let them return home. I waited till all the tumult of their departure was over, then I, too, silently lifted my hat in a last 'farewell.' It was quite noon then, and the grave lay in a band of sunshine—a very pleasant grave to remember, Elizabeth."

She was weeping unrestrainedly, and Richard let her weep. Such rain softens and fertilizes the soul, and leaves a harvest of blessedness behind. And when the first shock was over, Elizabeth could almost rejoice for the dead; for Antony's life had been set to extremes—great ambitions and great failures—and few, indeed, are the spirits so finely touched as to walk with even balance between them. Therefore for the mercy that had released him from the trials and temptations of life, there was gratitude to be given, for it was due.

That night, when Martha brought in Elizabeth's candle, she said: "Martha, my brother is dead. Master Harry is now the young squire. You will see that this is understood by every one."

"God love him! And may t' light o' *his* countenance be forever on him!"

"And if any ask about Mr. Antony, you may say that he died in Texas."

"That is where Mrs. Millard lives?"

"Yes, Mrs. Millard lives in Texas. Mr. Antony died of consumption. O, Martha! sit down, I must tell you all about him;" and Elizabeth went over the pitiful story, and talked about it, until both women were weary with weeping. The next morning they hung Antony's picture between that of his father and mother. It had been taken just after his return from college, in the very first glory of his youthful manhood, and Elizabeth looked fondly at it, and linked it only with memories of their happy innocent childhood, and with the grand self-abnegation of "the dead man's journey."

The news of Antony's death caused a perceptible reaction in popular feeling. The young man, after a hard struggle with adverse fate, had paid the last debt, and the great debt. Good men refrain from judging those who have gone to God's tribunal. Even his largest creditors evinced a disposition to take, with consideration, their claim, as the estate could pay it; and some willingness to allow at last, "thet Miss Hallam hed done t' right thing." The fact of the Whaley Brothers turning her defenders rather confounded them. They had a profound respect for "t' Whaleys;" and if "t' Whaleys were for backin' up Miss Hallam's ways," the majority were sure that Miss Hallam's ways were such as commended themselves to "men as stood firm for t' law and t' land o' England." With any higher test they did not trouble themselves.

The public recognition of young Harry Hallam as the future squire also gave great satisfaction. After all, no stranger and foreigner was to have rule over them; for Richard they certainly regarded in that light. "He might be a Hallam to start wi'," said Peter Crag, "but he's been that way mixed up wi' French and such, thet t' Hallam in him is varry hard to find." All the tenants, upon the advent of Richard, had stood squarely upon their dignity; they had told each other that they'd pay rent only to a Hallam, and they had quite determined to resent any suggestion made by Richard, and to disregard any order he gave.

But it was quickly evident that Richard did not intend to take any more interest in Hallam than he did in the Church glebe and tithes, and that the only thing he desired was the bride he had waited so long for. The spring was far advanced, however, before the wedding-day was fixed; for there was much to provide for, and many things to arrange, in view of the long-continued absences which would be almost certain. The Whaleys, urged by a lover, certainly hurried their work to a degree which astonished all their subordinates; but yet February had passed before all the claims against Antony Hallam had been collected. The debt, as debt always is, was larger than had been expected; and twelve years' income would be exhausted in its liquidation. Elizabeth glanced at Harry and looked gravely at the papers; but Richard said, "Be satisfied, dear. He will have the income at the age he really needs it—when he begins his university career—until then we can surely care for him."

So Hallam was left, financially, in the Whaleys' care. They were to collect all its revenues, and keep the house and grounds in repair, and, after paying all expenses incidental to this duty, they were to divide, in fair proportions, the balance every three years among Antony's creditors. This arrangement gave perfect satisfaction, for, as Marmaduke Halcroft said, "If t' Whaleys ar'n't to be trusted, t' world might as well stand still, and let honest men get out o' it."

As to the house, it was to be left absolutely in Martha's care. Inside its walls her authority was to be undisputed, and Elizabeth insisted that her salary should be on the most liberal basis. In fact, Martha's position made her a person of importance—a woman who could afford to do handsomely toward her chapel, and who might still have put by a large sum every year.

The wedding was a very pretty one, and Elizabeth, in her robe of white satin and lace, with pearls around her throat and arms, was a most lovely bride. Twelve young girls, daughters of her tenants, dressed in white, and carrying handfuls of lilies-of-the-valley, went with her to the altar; and Richard had for his attendant the handsome little squire. The rector took the place of Elizabeth's father, and a neighboring clergyman performed the ceremony. Most of the surrounding families were present in the church, and with this courtesy Elizabeth was quite satisfied. Immediately after the marriage they left for Liverpool, and when they arrived at Richard's home it was in the time of orange blooms and building birds, as he had desired it should be, six years before.

But one welcome which they would gladly have heard was wanting. Bishop Elliott had removed, and no other preacher had taken his place in Richard's home. This was caused, however, by the want of some womanly influence as a conductor. It was Phyllis who had brought the kindred souls together, and made pleasant places for them to walk and talk in. Phyllis had desired very much to meet Elizabeth, on her advent into her American life, but the time had been most uncertain, and so many other duties held the wife and mother and mistress, that it had been thought better to defer the pleasure till it could be more definitely arranged. And then, after all, it was Elizabeth that went to see Phyllis. One day Richard came home in a hurry.

"Elizabeth! I am going to Texas — to Austin. Suppose you and Harry go with me. We will give Phyllis a surprise."

"But housekeepers don't like surprises, Richard."

"Then we will write before leaving, but I doubt if the letter will be in advance of us."

It was not. John Millard's home was a couple of miles distant from Austin, and the mail was not gone for with any regularity. Besides, at this time, John was attending to his duties in the Legislature, and Phyllis relied upon his visits to the post-office.

It was a pleasant afternoon in June when the stage deposited them in the beautiful city, and after some refreshment Richard got a buggy and determined to drive out to the Millard place. Half a mile distant from it they met a boy about seven years old on a mustang, and Richard asked him if he could direct him to Captain Millard's house.

"I reckon so," said the little chap, with a laugh; "I generally stop there, if I'm not on horseback."

"O, indeed! What is your name?"

"My name is Richard Millard. What's your name, sir?"

"My name is Richard Fontaine; and I shouldn't wonder if you are my nephew."

"I'm about certain you are my uncle. And is that my English aunt? Wont ma be glad? Say, wont you hurry up? I was going into the city. My pa's going to speak to-night. Did you ever hear my pa speak?"

"No; but I should like to do so."

"I should think you would. See! There's ma.

That is Lulu hanging on to her, and that is Sam Houston in her arms. My pony is called 'San Jacinto.' Say! Who is that with you and aunt, Uncle Richard? I mean *you;* " and he nodded and smiled at Harry.

"That is Harry Hallam—a relation of yours."

"I'm glad of that. Would he like to ride my pony?"

"Yes," answered Harry, promptly.

But Richard declined to make exchanges just there, especially as they could see Phyllis curiously watching their approach. In another moment she had given Sam Houston to a negro nurse, flung a sun-bonnet on her head, and was tripping to the gate to meet them.

"O how glad I am, Elizabeth! I knew you the minute I saw the tip of your hat, Richard! And this is Harry Hallam! Come in, come in; come with ten thousand welcomes!"

What a merry household it was! What a joyous, plentiful, almost out-of-doors meal was ready in half an hour! And then, as soon as the sun set, Phyllis said, "Now, if you are not tired, we will go and surprise John. He is to speak to-night, and I make a point of listening to him, in the capitol."

Richard and Elizabeth were pleased with the proposal; but Harry desired to stay with young Millard. The boys had fraternized at once,—what good boys do not? especially when there are ponies and rabbits and puppies and pigeons to exhibit, and talk about.

Phyllis had matured into a very beautiful woman, and Richard was proud of both his sister and his wife, when he entered the Texas capitol with them. It was a stirring scene he saw, and certainly a gathering of manhood of a very exceptional character. The lobbies were full of lovely, brilliant women; and scattered among them—chatting, listening, love-making—was many a well-known hero, on whose sun-browned face the history of Texas was written. The matter in dispute did not much interest Elizabeth, but she listened with amusement to a conversation between Phyllis and pretty Betty Lubbock about the latter's approaching wedding, and her trip to the "States."

In the middle of a description of the bridal dress, there fell upon her ears these words: "A bill for the relief of the Millard Rangers." She looked eagerly to see who would rise. It was only a prosy old man who opposed the measure, on the ground that the State could not afford to protect such a far-outlying frontier.

"Perish the State that cannot protect her citizens!" cried a vehement voice from another seat, and forthwith leaped to his feet Captain John Millard. Elizabeth had never seen him, but she knew, from Phyllis's sudden silence, and the proud light in her face, who it was. He talked as he fought, with all his soul, a very Rupert in debate, as he was in battle. In three minutes all whispering had ceased; women listened with full eyes, men with glowing cheeks; and when he sat down the bill was virtually passed by acclamation. Phyllis was silently weeping, and not, perhaps, altogether for the slaughtered women and children on the frontier; there were a few proud, happy tears for interests nearer home.

Then came John's surprise, and the happy ride home, and many and many a joyful day after it—a month of complete happiness, of days devoid of care, and filled with perfect love and health and friendship, and made beautiful with the sunshine and airs of an earthly paradise. Phyllis's home was a roomy wooden house, spreading wide, as every thing does in Texas, with doors and windows standing open, and deep piazzas on every side. Behind it was a grove of the kingly magnolia, in front the vast shadows of the grand pecans. Greenest turf was under them; and there was, besides, a multitude of flowers, and vines which trailed up the lattices of the piazzas, and over the walls and roofs, and even dropped in at the chamber windows.

There was there, also, the constant stir of happy servants, laughing and singing at their work, of playing children, of trampling horses, of the coming and going of guests; for Captain Millard's house was near a great highway, and was known far and wide for its hospitality. The stranger fastened his horse at the fence, and asked undoubtingly for a cup of coffee, or a glass of milk, and Phyllis had a pleasant word and a cheerful meal for every caller; so that John rarely wanted company when he sat in the cool and silence of the evening. It might be a ranger from the Pecos, or a trader from the Rio Grande, or a land speculator from the States, or an English gentleman on his travels, or a Methodist missionary doing his circuit; yea, sometimes half a dozen travelers and sojourners met together there, and then they talked and argued and described until the "night turned," and the cocks were crowing for the dawning.

Richard thoroughly enjoyed the life, and Elizabeth's nature expanded in it, as a flower in sunshine. What gallops she had on the prairies! What rambles with Phyllis by the creek sides in search of strange flowers! What sweet confidences! What new experiences! What a revelation altogether of a real, fresh, natural life it was! And she saw with her own eyes, and with a kind of wonder, the men who had dared to be free, and to found a republic of free men in the face of nine million Mexicans—men of iron wills, who under rude felt hats had the finest heads, and under buckskin vests the warmest hearts. Phyllis was always delighted to point them out, to tell over again their exploits, and to watch the kindling of the heroic fire in Elizabeth's eyes.

It was, indeed, a wonderful month, and the last

day of it was marked by a meeting that made a deep impression upon Elizabeth. She was dressing in the afternoon when she heard a more than usually noisy arrival. Looking out of the window she saw a man unsaddling his horse, and a crowd of negroes running to meet him. It seemed, also, as if every one of John's forty-two dogs was equally delighted at the visit. Such a barking! Such a chorus of welcome! Such exclamations of satisfaction it is impossible to describe. The new-comer was a man of immense stature, evidently more used to riding than to walking. For his gait was slouching, his limbs seemed to dangle about him, and he had a lazy, listless stoop, as he came up the garden with his saddle over his arm, listening to a score of voices, patting the dogs that leaped around and upon him, stopping to lift up a little negro baby that had toddled between his big legs and fallen, and, finally, standing to shake hands with Uncle Isaac, the patriarch of The Quarters. And as Uncle Isaac never—except after long absences—paid even "Master John" the honor of coming to meet him, Elizabeth wondered who the guest could be.

Coming down stairs she met Harriet in her very gayest head-kerchief and her white-embroidered apron and her best-company manner: "De minister am come, Miss Lizzie—de Rev. Mr. Rollins am 'rived; and de camp-meetin' will be 'ranged 'bout now. I'se powerful sorry you kaint stay, ma'am."

"Where does Mr. Rollins come from?"

"De Lord knows whar. He's at de Rio Grande, and den 'fore you can calc'late he's at de Colorado."

"He appears to be a great favorite."

"He's done got de hearts ob ebery one in his right hand; and de dogs! dey whimper after him for a week; and de little children! he draw dem to him from dar mammy's breast. Nobody's never seed sich a man!"

He was talking to John when Elizabeth went on the gallery, and Harry was standing between his knees, and Dick Millard leaning on his shoulder. Half a dozen of the more favored dogs were lying around him, and at least a dozen negro children were crawling up the piazza steps, or peeping through the railings. He was dressed in buckskin and blue flannel, and at first sight had a most unclerical look. But the moment he lifted his face Elizabeth saw what a clear, noble soul looked out from the small twinkling orbs beneath his large brows. And as he grew excited in the evening's conversation, his muscles nerved, his body straightened, and he became the wiry, knotted embodiment of calm power and determination.

"We expected you two weeks ago," said John to him.

"There was work laid out for me I hadn't calcu-lated on, John. Bowie's men were hard up for fresh meat, and I lent them my rifle a few days. Then the Indians bothered me. They were hanging around

Saledo settlement in a way I didn't like, so I watched them until I was about sure of their next dirty trick. It happened to be a thieving one on the Zavala ranche, so I let Zavala know, and then rode on to tell Granger he'd better send a few boys to keep them red-handed Comanche from picking and stealing and murdering."

"It was just like you. You probably saved many lives."

"Saving life is often saving souls, John. Next time I go that way every man at Zavala's ranche and every man in Granger's camp will listen to me. I shall then have a greater danger than red men to tell them of. But they know both my rifle and my words are true, and when I say to them, 'Boys, there's hell and heaven right in your path, and your next step may plunge you into the fiery gulf, or open to you the golden gates,' they'll listen to me, and they'll believe me. John, it takes a soldier to preach to soldiers, and a saved sinner to know how to save other sinners."

"And if report is not unjust," said Richard, "you will find plenty of great sinners in such circuits as you take."

"Sir, you'll find sinners, great sinners, everywhere. I acknowledge that Texas has been made a kind of receptacle for men too wicked to live among their fellows. I often come upon these wild, carrion jail-birds. I know them a hundred yards off. It is a great thing, every way, that they come here. God be thanked! Texas has nothing to fear from them. In the first place, though the atmosphere of crime is polluting in a large city, it infects nobody here. I tell you, sir, the murderer on a Texas prairie is miserable. There is nothing so terrible to him as this freedom and loneliness, in which he is always in the company of his outraged conscience, which drives him hither and thither, and gives him no rest. For I tell you, that murderers don't willingly meet together, not even over the whisky bottle. They know each other, and shun each other. Well, sir, this subject touches me warmly at present, for I am just come from the death-bed of such a man. I have been with him three days. You remember Bob Black, John?"

"Yes. A man who seldom spoke, and whom no one liked. A good soldier, though. I don't believe he knew the meaning of fear."

"Didn't he? I have seen him sweat with terror. He has come to me more dead than alive, clung to my arms like a child, begged me to stand between him and the shapes that followed him."

"Drunk?"

"No, sir. I don't think he ever tasted liquor; but he was a haunted man! He had been a sixfold murderer, and his victims made life a terror to him."

"How do you account for that?"

"We have a spiritual body, and we have a natural

body. When it pleases the Almighty, he opens the eyes and ears of our spiritual body, either for comfort, or advice, or punishment. This criminal saw things and heard words no mortal eyes have perceived, nor mortal ears understood. The man was haunted. I cannot doubt it."

"I believe what you say," said Elizabeth, solemnly, "for I have heard, and I have seen."

"And so have I," said the preacher, in a kind of rapture. "When I lay sleeping on the St. Mark's one night, I felt the thrill of a mighty touch, and I heard, with my spiritual ears, words which no mortal lips uttered; and I rose swiftly, and saved my life from the Comanche by the skin of my teeth. And another night, as I rode over the Maverick prairie, when it was knee-deep in grass and flowers, and the stars were gathering one by one with a holy air into the house of God, I could not restrain myself, and I sang aloud for joy! Then, suddenly, there seemed to be all around me a happy company, and my spiritual ears were opened, and I heard a melody beyond the voices of earth, and I was not ashamed in it of my little human note of praise. I tell you, death only sets us face to face with Him who is not very far from us at any time."

"And Bob is dead?"

"Yes; and I believe he is saved."

No one spoke; and the preacher, after a minute's silence, asked, "Who doubts?"

"A sixfold murderer, you said?"

"Nay, nay, John; are you going to limit the grace of God? Do you know the height and depth of his mercy? Have you measured the length and breadth of the cross? I brought the cross of Christ to that fiend-haunted bed, and the wretched soul clasped it, clung to it, yes, climbed up by it into heaven!"

"It was peace at last, then?" said Phyllis.

"It was triumph! The devil lost all power to torture him; for, with the sweet assurance of his forgiveness came the peace that passeth understanding. What is there for great criminals? Only the cross of Christ? O the miracle of love, that found out for us such an escape!"

"And you think that the man really believed himself to be forgiven by God?"

"I am sure that he knew he was forgiven."

"It is wonderful. Why, then, do not all Christians have this knowledge?"

"It is their privilege to have it; but how few of us have that royal nature which claims all our rights! The cross of Christ! There are still Jewish minds to whom it is a stumbling-block; and still more minds of the Greek type to whom it is foolishness."

"But is not this doctrine specially a Methodist one?"

"If St. Paul was a Methodist, and St. Augustine, and Martin Luther, and the millions of saved men, to whom God has counted 'faith' in his word and mercy 'for righteousness,' then it is specially Methodist. What says the Lord? 'Therefore being justified by faith, we have peace with God, through our Lord Jesus Christ.' I do not say but what there are many good men without this assurance; but I do say, that it is the privilege of all who love and *believe* God. John Wesley himself did not experience this joy until he heard the Moravian, Peter Bohler, preach. 'Before that,' he says, 'I was a servant of God, accepted and safe, but now I *knew it*.'"

Elizabeth did not again reply. She sat very still, her hand clasped in that of Phyllis, whose head was leaning upon her breast. And very frequently she glanced down at the pale, spiritual face with its luminous dark eyes and sweet mouth. For Phyllis had to perfection that lovely, womanly charm, which puts itself *en rapport* with every mood, and yet only offers the sympathy of a sensitive silence and an answering face.

As the women sat musing the moon rose, and then up sprang the night breeze, laden with the perfume of bleaching grass, and all the hot, sweet scents of the south.

"How beautiful is this land!" said Richard, in an enthusiasm. "What a pity the rabble of other lands cannot be kept out of it!"

The preacher lifted his head with a quick belligerent motion: "There is no such thing as rabble, sir. For the meanest soul Christ paid down his precious blood. What you call 'rabble' are the builders of kingdoms and nationalities."

"Yes," said John, "I dare say if we could see the fine fellows who fought at Hastings, and those who afterward forced Magna Charta from King John without the poetic veil of seven hundred years, we should be very apt to call them 'rabble' also. Give the founders of Texas the same time, and they may also have a halo round their heads. Was not Rome founded by robbers, and Great Britain by pirates?"

"There is work for every man, and men for every work. These 'rabble,' under proper leaders, were used by the Almighty for a grand purpose—the redemption of this fair land, and his handful of people in it, from the thrall of the priests of Rome. Would such men as the Livingstons, the Carrolls, the Renselaers, or the wealthy citizens of Philadelphia or Washington have come here and fought Indians and Mexicans; and been driven about from pillar to post, living on potatoes and dry corn? Good respectable people suffer a great deal of tyranny ere they put their property in danger. But when Texas, in her desperation, rose, she was glad of the men with a brand on their body and a rope round their neck, and who did not value their lives more than an empty nut-shell. They did good service. Many of them won back fair names and men's respect and God's love. I call no man 'rabble.' I know that many of these outcasts thanked God for an opportunity to offer their lives for the general good," and, he added, dropping his voice almost to a whisper, "I know of instances where the sacrifice was accepted, and assurance of that acceptance granted."

"The fight for freedom seems to be a never-ending one."

"Because," said the preacher, "Man was created free. Freedom is his birthright, even though he be born in a prison, and in chains. Hence, the noblest men are not satisfied with physical and political freedom; they must also be free men in Christ Jesus; for let me tell you, if men are slaves to sin and the devil, not all the Magna Chartas, nor all the swords in the world, can make them truly free."

And thus they talked until the moon set and the last light was out in the cabins, and the 'after midnight' feeling became plainly evident. Then Phyllis brought out a dish that looked very like walnut shells, but which all welcomed. They were preserved bears' paws. "Eat," she said, "for though it is the last hour we may meet in this life, we must sleep now."

And the Texan luxury was eaten with many a pleasant word, and then, with kind and solemn 'farewells,' the little party separated, never in all the years of earth to sit together again; for just at daylight, John and Phyllis stood at their gates, watching the carriage which carried Richard and Elizabeth pass over the hill, and into the timber, and out of sight.

CHAPTER XI.

"The evening of life brings with it its lamp."—TOUBERT.

"And there arrives a lull in the hot race:
And an unwonted calm pervades the breast.
And then he thinks he knows
The hills where his life rose,
And the sea, where it goes."—ARNOLD.

"She has passed
To where, beyond these voices, there is peace."

IT is the greatest folly to think that the only time worth writing about is youth. It is an equal folly to imagine that love is the only passion universally interesting. Elizabeth's years were no less vivid, no less full of feeling and of changes, after her marriage than before it. Indeed, she never quite lost the interests of her maiden life. Hallam demanded an oversight she did not fail to give it. Three times during the twelve years of its confiscation to Antony's creditors she visited it. In these visits she was accompanied by Richard, and Harry, and her own children. Then the Whaleys' accounts were carefully gone over, and found always to be perfectly honorable and satisfactory. And it is needless to say how happy Martha was at such times.

Gradually all ill-feeling passed away. The young squire, though educated abroad, had just such a training as made him popular. For he passed part of every year in Texas with Dick Millard, and all that could be known about horses and hunting and woodcraft, Harry Hallam knew. He had also taken on very easily the Texan manner, frank, yet rather proud and phlegmatic: "Evidently a young man who knows what he wants, and will be apt to get it," said Whaley.

"Nine Yorkshire jockeys knocked into one couldn't blind him on a horse," said young Horton.

"And I'll lay a guinea he'll lead in every hunting field."

"And they do say, he's a first-rate scholar besides."

Such conversations regarding him were indefinitely repeated, and varied.

When he was in his eighteenth year the estate was absolutely free of every claim, and in a condition which reflected the greatest credit upon those in whose care it had been placed. It was at this time that Richard and Elizabeth took the young man into his grandfather's room, and laid before him the title deeds of his patrimony and the schedule of its various incomes. Then, also, they told him, with infinite kindness and forbearance, the story of his father's efforts and failures, and the manner in which the estate had been handled, so that it might be made over to him free of all debt and stain.

Harry said very little. His adopted parents liked him the better for that. But he was profoundly amazed and grateful. Then he went to Cambridge, and for three years Elizabeth did not see him. It had been arranged, however, that the whole family should meet at Hallam on the anniversary of his majority, and the occurrence was celebrated with every public festivity that had always attended that event in the Hallam family. There was nothing to dim the occasion. Every one, far and near, took the opportunity to show that ill-thoughts and ill-feelings were forever buried, and Elizabeth and Richard were feted with especial honor.

"Few women would hev done so well by t' land and t' family," admitted even Lord Eltham, "and if I wasn't so old and feeble, I'd go and tell her so; and to be foreign-born, that Mr. Fontaine has been varry square, that he hes. He shows t' English blood in him."

"Ay, it's hard to wear Yorkshire out. It bears a deal o' waterin', and is still strong and straightfor'ard," answered Whaley.

"Now he'll hev to wed and settle down."

"He'll do that. I've seen a deal o' him, and I've noticed that he has neither eyes nor ears but for our little lass, a varry bonny lass she is!"

"It 'll be Alice Horton, happen?"

"Nay, it isn't. It's his cousin, Bessie Fontaine. She's but a girl yet, but she's t' varry image o' her mother, just what Elizabeth Hallam was at sixteen—happen only a bit slighter and more delicate-looking."

"And no wonder, Whaley. To be brought up i' a place like that New Orleans. Wyh-a! they do say that t' winter weather there is like our haymakin' time! Poor thing! She'll get a bit o' color here, I'se warrant."

The Yorkshire lawyer had seen even into a love affair with clear eyes. Bessie and Harry had already confided their affection to Elizabeth, but she was quite determined that there should be no engagement until after Harry returned from a three-years' travel in Europe and Asia.

"Then, Harry," she said, "you will have seen the women of many lands. And Bessie will also have seen something of the world, and of the society around her. She must choose you from among all others, and not simply because habit and contiguity and family relations have thrown you together."

Still it pleased her, that from every part of the world came regularly and constantly letters and tokens of Harry's love for her daughter. She would not force, she would not even desire, such a consummation; but yet, if a true and tried affection should unite the cousins, it would be a wonderful settlement of that succession which had so troubled and perplexed her father, and which at last he had humbly left to the wisdom and direction of a higher Power.

Therefore, when Harry, in his twenty-fourth year, browned and bearded with much travel, came back to

New Orleans, to ask the hand of the only woman he had ever loved, Elizabeth was very happy. Her daughter was going back to her old home, going to be the mistress of its fair sunny rooms, and renew in her young life the hopes and memories of a by-gone generation.

And to the happy bridal came John and Phyllis, and all their handsome sons and daughters, and never was there a more sweetly, solemn marriage-feast. For many wise thoughts had come to Elizabeth as her children grew up at her side, and one of them was a conviction that marriage is too sacred a thing to be entered into amid laughter and dancing and thoughtless feasting. "If Jesus was asked to the marriage, as he was in Cana of Galilee, there would be fewer unhappy marriages," she said. So the young bride was sent away with smiles and kisses and loving joyful wishes, but not in a whirl of dancing and champagne gayety and noisy selfish merriment.

And the years came and went, and none of them were alike. In one, it was the marriage of her eldest son, Richard, to Lulu Millard; in another, the death of a baby girl very dear to her. She had her daily crosses and her daily blessings, and her daily portion of duties. But in the main, it may be said, for Richard and Elizabeth Fontaine, that they had "borne the yoke in their youth," and learned the great lessons of life, before the days came in which their strength began to fail them.

The last year of any life may generally be taken as the verdict upon that life. Elizabeth's was a very happy one. She was one of those women on whom time lays a consecrating hand. Her beauty, in one sense, had gone; in another sense, she was fairer than ever. Her noble face had lost its bloom and its fine contour, but her mouth was sweeter and stronger, and her eyes full of the light of a soul standing in the promise of heaven. She had much of her old energy and activity. In the spring of the year she went to Texas to see a son and daughter who had settled there; and, with one of her grandchildren, rode thoughtfully, but not unhappily, over all the pleasant places she had been with Richard that first happy year of their marriage. Richard had been six years dead, but she had never mourned him as those mourn who part hands in mid-life, when the way is still long before the lonely heart. In a short time they would meet again, for

> "As the pale waste widens around us,
>   And the banks fade dimmer away,
> As the stars come out, the night wind
>   Brings up the stream
> Murmurs and scents of the infinite sea."

Yet there had been a very solemn parting between her and Phyllis; and when Phyllis stooped twice to the face in the departing carriage, and the two women kissed each other so silently, John was somehow touched into an unusual thoughtfulness; and for the first time realized that his sweet Phyllis was fading away. He could not talk in his usual cheery manner, and when he said, "Farewell, Elizabeth," and held her hand, he involuntarily glanced at his wife, and walked away with his eyes full of tears.

But as the brain grows by knowledge, so the heart is made larger by loving; and Elizabeth was rich and happy in the treasures she had garnered. The past no prayer could bring back; the future she counted not; but she enjoyed in every hour the blessing they brought her. The voyage across the ocean was delightful; she found young hearts to counsel, and aged ones to change experiences with. Every one desired to talk to her, and counted it a favor to sit or to walk by her side. So beautiful is true piety; so lovely is the soul that comes into daily life fresh from the presence of the Deity.

She had left Texas in May; she arrived at Hallam in June. And how beautiful the dear old place was! But Martha had gone to her reward two years previously, and Elizabeth missed her. She had lived to be eighty-eight years old, and had not so much died as fallen asleep. She had never left the hall, but, as long as she was able, had taken charge of all its treasures and of every thing concerning the children. Even when confined to her room, they had come to her with their troubles and their joys, and her fingers were busy for them unto the last day.

Yet no one missed Martha as Elizabeth missed her.

With Martha she talked on subjects she mentioned to no one else. They had confidences no others could share. It seemed as if the last link which bound her to her youth was broken. But one morning, as her daughter was slowly driving her through Hallam village, she saw an old man who had been very pleasantly linked with the by-gone years, and she said, "That is a very dear friend, I must speak to him, Bessie."

He was a slight old man, with thin hair white as wool falling on his shoulders, and a face full of calm contemplation. "Mr. North," said Elizabeth, tremulously, "do you remember me?"

He removed his hat, and looked attentively in the face bending toward him. Then, with a smile, "Ah, yes, I remember Miss Hallam. God is good to let me see you again. I am very glad, indeed."

"You must come to the hall with me, if you can; I have a great deal to say to you."

And thus it happened that after this meeting Bessie frequently stopped for him in the village, and that gradually he spent more and more time at the hall. There he always occupied the large room called the "Chamber of Peace," hallowed by the memory of the apostle of his faith.

One hot August day he had gone to its cool, calm shelter, after spending an hour with Elizabeth. Their conversation had been in heaven, and specially of the early dead and blessed, who went in the serenity of the morning; whose love for God had known no treachery, and who took the hand of Jesus and followed him with all their heart.

"I think theirs will be the radiant habitations, and the swift obedience of the seraphim. They will know and love and work, as do the angels."

"In middle life," said Elizabeth, "heaven seems farther away from us."

"True, my sister. At midday the workman may think of the evening, but it is his work that chiefly engrosses him. Not that the Christian ever forgets God in his labor, but he needs to be on the alert, and to keep every faculty busy. But when the shades of evening gather, he begins to think of going home, and of the result of his labor."

"In middle life, too, death amazes us. In the moment of hearing of such a death I always found my heart protest against it. But as I grow older I can feel that all the cords binding to life grow slack. How will it be at the end?"

"I think as soon as heaven is seen, we shall tend toward it. We will not go away in sadness, dear sister; we shall depart in the joy of his salvation. If I was by your side, I should not say, "Farewell;" I should speak of our meeting again."

Then he went away, and Elizabeth, with a happy face, drew her chair to the open window of her room and lifted her work. It was a piece of silken patch-work, made of dresses and scarfs and sashes, that each had a history in her memory. There were circles from Phyllis's and her own wedding dresses, one from a baby sash of her son Charles. Charles hung his sword from a captain's belt then, but she kept the blue ribbon of his babyhood. There was a bit from Jack's first cravat, and Dick's flag, and her dear husband's wedding vest, and from the small silken shoes of the little Maya—dear little Maya, who

> "From the nursery door,
> Climbed up with clay cold feet
> Unto the golden floor."

Any wife and mother can imagine the thousand silken strips that would gather in a life of love.

She had often said that in her old age she would sew together these memorials of her sorrow and her joy; and Bessie frequently stood beside her, listening to events which this or that piece called forth, and watching the gay beautiful squares, as they grew in the summer sunshine and by the glinting winter firelight.

After Mr. North left her she lifted her work and sat sewing and singing. It was an unusually hot day; the perfume from the August lilies and the lavender and the rich carnations almost made the heart faint. All the birds were still; but the bees were busy, and far off there was the soft tinkling of the water falling into the two fountains on the terrace. Harry came in, and said, "I am going into Hallam, mother, so I kiss you before I go;" and she rose up and kissed the handsome fellow, and watched him away, and when he turned and lifted his hat to her, she blessed him, and thanked God that he had let her live to see Antony's son so good and worthy an inheritor of the old name and place.

By and by her thoughts drifted westward to her son Charles, with his regiment on the Colorado plains, to her son Richard in his Texan home, to Phyllis and John, to her daughter Netta, to the graves of Richard and the little Maya. It seemed to her as if all her work was finished. How wonderfully the wrong had been put right! How worthy Harry was! How happy her own dear Bessie! If her father could see the home he had left with anxious fears, she thought he would be satisfied. "I shall be glad to see him," she said, softly; "he will say to me, 'Thou did right, Elizabeth!' I think that his praise will be sweet, even after the Master's."

At this point in her reflections Bessie came into her room. She had her arms full of myrtles and glowing dahlias, of every color; and she stooped and kissed her mother, and praised the beauty of her work, and then began to arrange the flowers in the large vases which stood upon the hearth and upon the table.

"It is a most beautiful day, mother! a most beautiful world! I wonder why God says he will make a new world! How can a new one be fairer?"

"His tabernacle will be in it, Bessie. Think of

that, my child. An intimate happiness with him. No more sin. All tears wiped away. Bessie, there may be grander worlds among the countless stars, but O earth! fair happy earth, that has such hope of heaven!" and she began to sing to the sweet old tune of "Immanuel,"

> "There is a land of pure delight,
> Where saints—"

There was a sudden pause, and Bessie lifted the strain, but ere the verse was finished, turned suddenly and looked at her mother. The next moment she was at her side. With the needle in her fingers, with the song upon her lips, Elizabeth had gone to "Immanuel's Land," without even a parting sigh.

It seemed almost wrong to weep for such a death. Bessie knelt praying by her mother's side, holding her hands, and gazing into the dear face, fast settling into those solemn curves which death makes firm and sharp-cut, as if they were to endure for ages, until the transition was quite complete. Then she called in the old servants who most loved her mother, and they dressed her for her burial, and laid her upon the small, snowy bed which had been hers from her girlhood. And the children gathered the white odorous everlastings and the white flowers in all the garden, and with soft steps and tender hands spread them over the still breast, and the pure drapery. And when Mr. North came in with Harry, though

Harry wept, the preacher could not. With a face full of triumph, he looked at her, and said only, "Go in peace; soul beautiful and blessed!"

It had been well known for more than a year that Elizabeth's life was held at a moment's tenure. It was a little singular that Phyllis was suffering, also, from a complaint almost analogous; and when they had bid each other a farewell in the spring, they had understood it to be the last of earth. Indeed, Phyllis had whispered to Elizabeth in that parting moment, "I give you a rendezvous in heaven, my darling!"

Often also during the summer Bessie had heard her mother softly singing to herself:

> "I look unto the gates of His high place,
>   Beyond the sea;
> For I know he is coming shortly,
>   To summon me.
> And when a shadow falls across the window
>   Of my room,
> Where I am working my appointed task,
> I lift my head to watch the door, and ask
>   If he is come?
> And the Angel answers sweetly,
>   In my home,
> Only a few more shadows,
>   And he will come."

She was laid with her fathers in the old church-yard at Hallam. And O, how sweet is the sleep of those whom the King causeth to rest! Neither lands nor houses nor gold, nor yet the joy of a fond and faithful lover, tempted Elizabeth Hallam to leave the path of honor and rectitude; but when her trial was finished, bear witness how God blessed her! giving her abundantly of all good things in this life, and an inheritance, incorruptible, undefiled, and which shall never pass away from her.

THE END.

www.ingramcontent.com/pod-product-compliance
Lightning Source LLC
Chambersburg PA
CBHW030746250426
43672CB00028B/1072